MIXED MARTIAL ARTS
FIGHTING TECHNIQUES

DANNY INDIO

TUTTLE Publishing

Tokyo | Rutland, Vermont | Singapore

Acknowledgments

I dedicate this book to my father and mother who gave me love and discipline, and encouraged me while keeping me grounded.

Acknowledgment is made to all of my family, including my brothers: Gustavo, Fraise, Umberto, Norberto, and in particular, Ivan; my sisters: Gladys, Anna and Alfa; my brothers-in-law: Anibal and Altaf; my friends: Danny and Jose; and my wonderful nephews and nieces: Givaily, Daniel, Samantha, Sarah, Lauren, Shaely and Gabriel. Also to Sifu Danny Anderson and his instructors: Phil Cruz, Yeydy de la Cruz, Chuck Figueroa, Dwight Grant, Gerald Cruz, Gus Heisey, Pablo Vasquez, Anson Davis; plus fellow warriors: Terrence McCall, Jacques Pereira, Rogelio Castillo, Djinji Brown, Jay Patel, Paul Ochoa and all those who've helped me improve. I want to thank the master Guro Dan Inosanto for his work to keep Jeet Kune Do alive, as well as Paul Vunak, Tom Cruse, El Khattab Abdel "Krim," Shaolin Ribeiro, Tuhon McGrath, Salim Asli and all those who advance the martial arts. I acknowledge the USMC, where I learned to be a warrior. I'd like to thank all of the men and women in the armed services who put themselves on the line every day. Finally, to Sijo Bruce Lee: thanks to your vision, I am a fighter.

Published by Tuttle Publishing, an imprint of Periplus Editions (HK) Ltd.

www.tuttlepublishing.com

Copyright © 2012 by Danny Indio

Library of Congress Cataloging-in-Publication Data
Indio, Danny.
  Mixed martial arts fighting techniques : apply the modern training methods used by mma pros! / by Danny Indio.
    p. cm.
  ISBN 978-0-8048-4113-9 (pbk.)
1. Mixed martial arts. 2. Mixed martial arts--Training. I. Title.
  GV1102.7.M59I53 2012
  796.8--dc22
                  2011006677
ISBN 978-0-8048-4113-9

Distributed By

North America, Latin America & Europe
Tuttle Publishing
364 Innovation Drive
North Clarendon
VT 05759-9436 U.S.A.
Tel: 1 (802) 773-8930
Fax: 1 (802) 773-6993
info@tuttlepublishing.com
www.tuttlepublishing.com

Japan
Tuttle Publishing
Yaekari Building, 3rd Floor
5-4-12 Osaki, Shinagawa-ku
Tokyo 141 0032
Tel: (81) 3 5437-0171
Fax: (81) 3 5437-0755
sales@tuttle.co.jp
www.tuttle.co.jp

Asia Pacific
Berkeley Books Pte. Ltd.
61 Tai Seng Avenue #02-12
Singapore 534167
Tel: (65) 6280-1330
Fax: (65) 6280-6290
inquiries@periplus.com.sg
www.periplus.com

First edition
16 15 14 13 12
6 5 4 3 2 1   1110EP
Printed in Hong Kong

The Tuttle Story
"Books to Span the East and West"

Most people are very surprised to learn that the world's largest publisher of books on Asia had its beginnings in the tiny American state of Vermont. The company's founder, Charles E. Tuttle, belonged to a New England family steeped in publishing. And his first love was naturally books—especially old and rare editions.

Immediately after WW II, serving in Tokyo under General Douglas MacArthur, Tuttle was tasked with reviving the Japanese publishing industry, and founded the Charles E. Tuttle Publishing Company, which still thrives today as one of the world's leading independent publishers.

Though a westerner, Charles was hugely instrumental in bringing a knowledge of Japan and Asia to a world hungry for information about the East. By the time of his death in 1993, Tuttle had published over 6,000 titles on Asian culture, history and art—a legacy honored by the Japanese emperor with the "Order of the Sacred Treasure," the highest tribute Japan can bestow upon a non-Japanese.

With a backlist of 1,500 books, Tuttle Publishing is as active today as at any time in its past—inspired by Charles' core mission to publish fine books to span the East and West and provide a greater understanding of each.

Contents

Preface

This book is an attempt to distill the most effective self-defense methods for the street that a mixed martial artist would need to use outside of the ring. After over ten years of training and competing, primarily in Jeet Kune Do, I'm reminded time and again of how the simplest solution is usually the best solution. I discovered Jeet Kune Do a couple of years after watching the first UFC in 1993. Like many others during that time, I felt that mixed martial arts was the answer to my quest for a complete, true fighting art. Accordingly, I searched for a school that taught striking and grappling arts under the umbrella of mixed martial arts. What I discovered in Jeet Kune Do was everything that I was looking for and more. I learned all the different forms of fighting that I would need for the ring but furthermore; I learned all of the fighting techniques I would need for the street. Now, to be sure, the techniques you learn in boxing, Muay Thai and Brazilian Jiu Jitsu (and other arts like them) can serve you as well in a self-defense situation as they do in the ring, but it's as a result of a mental shift that needs to takes place. The mental shift in a self-defense streetfighting situation occurs as soon as you understand that, unlike in the ring, there are *no rules* in the streets. You apply combative techniques in the streets that you would not be able to do in the ring in a brutal, quick, and efficient manner.

Throughout the world, people train for a variety of reasons. For many, streetfighting self-defense is not their main reason to train. Yet a martial artist with a solid foundation in their techniques, good health, sharp attributes and a confident mind can adapt to the streetfighting scenario. Once a fighter senses that their life is in danger, they respond with "dirty" techniques as well as the techniques they've used in competition. As civilized people, we have an aversion to using "dirty" techniques when we fight because we feel that it is dishonorable to do so. But to fight outside of the ring is a dirty business, and it's always better to avoid a fight than to enter into a conflict with the mindset that you won't do certain techniques because they are "dishonorable." You can bet that your opponent won't have any such qualms. The key point is that we apply these "dirty" techniques when our life is in danger and there is no referee or anyone else around to stop the fight—we must do or we die. If one has to fight in the street, the main goal is to preserve one's life by stopping the opponent as soon as possible in the safest way possible. To do so requires that one prepare the mind beforehand for an encounter in the street, just as one prepares the mind before a fight in the ring.

Who Is This Book For?

Ultimately, this book is for everyone who wants to learn effective techniques for fighting and surviving on the streets. Fighters of all stripes will find something of use in this book: from the novice who is starting out in martial arts, to the experienced practitioner who wants additional combative techniques and concepts.

Introduction

"To understand combat one must approach it in a very simple and direct manner."
—*Bruce Lee*[1]

We rarely have the luxury of knowing when or where our next fight will be. For most of us that's because we're not looking to pick a fight in the streets. But it's good to know that you're ready for it when the time comes. When you train with simplicity and practicality in mind, then you know you can defend yourself with the most efficient and effective methods, concepts, and techniques. The popularity of mixed martial arts is the latest phenomenon that supports this conclusion.

Mixed martial arts echoes a common Bruce Lee maxim that says one should "absorb what is useful and disregard what is useless."[2] Also, directness, simplicity and effectiveness are concepts that the U.S. military advocates for fighting in armed and unarmed combat. As a result, the self-defense that the U.S. Army and the U.S. Marine Corps teaches their service members incorporates many techniques from the mixed martial arts world.

However, fighting in the ring and fighting outside of it are different arenas that, despite overlapping, require a crucial shift in techniques and strategy. They both incorporate many of the same techniques but with largely different aims. In the ring, you fight one individual in a matted and enclosed enviroment, according to set rules as guided by a referee so that you can win via points, knockout or submission. In the streets, you fight under usually unexpected circumstances against one or more individuals—who may or may not be armed—on rough and open terrain, with possible legal and mortal consequences. Even more extreme, if you're a soldier in a warzone, you are weighed down with military protective gear and carry a variety of weapons, surrounded by enemies from all sides who are also armed. Thus, every martial artist's development has to be adaptable to the type of enemy and situation they are likely to face. The great thing is that because many of the mixed martial arts techniques are efficient, simple and direct, they can be adapted to situations outside of the ring.

Like athletes, fighters are always pushing themselves to get better and be prepared to face all types of challenges. As the saying goes, "you fight the way you train"—you have to be adaptable and find time and ways to train in techniques outside of the typical ring scenario.

For example, we all know that an arm bar is a devastating weapon to use against any opponent. But should it be the first weapon you use in any given situation? As great as an arm bar might be in the ring, it would be of dubious benefit to use it as your "go-to move" in the streets where there are no mats and your opponent might have friends with him.

---

1   *Tao of Jeet Kune Do*, Bruce Lee
2   This is also attributed to Guru Dan Inosanto and Jiddu Krishnamurti

To fight effectively, the martial artist must be versatile enough to switch between lethal and nonlethal hand-to-hand combat techniques, whether he or she is armed or unarmed. Because this is a primer, the book will cover empty hand and knife techniques from the ranges of punching, kicking, clinching, takedowns and grappling.

A good martial artist always aims to develop his or her sensory awareness, decisiveness, accuracy, efficient use of their body and overall physical fitness. These basic elements should be constantly sharpened through meditation, visualization, study of all forms of martial arts, physical exercise, and individual martial arts training.

Sensory awareness calls for one to be constantly alert to the messages received through the senses; everything from smells in the air to the environment around us.

Decisiveness means one has a clear purpose to attack or defend, commits to their decision once it's made and uses good judgment to determine if he should attack or not.

Accuracy makes you better at hitting your target; this will help you end the fight quicker and increase your chances for survival.

Efficient use of your body means that you minimize wasteful physical motions and get to the target with the least amount of exertion for the maximum benefit.

Physical fitness necessarily involves pushing your body to improve its attributes, including: stamina, strength, speed, agility, flexibility and endurance.

The Jeet Kune Do Approach

Self-defense is a natural instinct. From a baby's reflexive kicking at an unwanted touch to our programmed fight-or-flight responses, we've had the self-defense survival instinct for as long as our species has been around. For thousands of years, all throughout the world, men have cultivated this instinct into formalized systems of self-defense complete with techniques, drills and exercises that build on our innate responses to form more effective and efficient methods. We are lucky, in this day and age, to be able to witness, learn and experience this culmination of martial wisdom and adopt what is most vital for our survival.

Hence, we see the growth of the sport of MMA as top competitors from different martial arts disciplines put their skills of kicking, punching, clinching and grappling to the test. Based on their successes and failures, they (and everyone else) then refine, correct, add to or improve on the techniques and strategies. It is a testament to Bruce Lee's vision of absorbing what is useful and disregarding what is useless that we strive to find the most efficient and effective techniques for our survival. And with the advances in technology, we now have access to this knowledge in the form of online video clips, comments in forums and countless magazine articles.

Because of its effective and efficient techniques with an emphasis on and combination of striking, clinching, takedowns, throws and grappling, MMA serves as one of the most complete martial arts today. This book provides a foundation of mixed martial arts techniques and strategies that every street fighter should know. Furthermore, the book expands on these basic striking, clinching, takedown and grappling techniques and adds methods and techniques that can allow a fighter to defend against knife-wielding attackers. As effective as MMA is in covering the many different forms of fighting, it overlooks the reality of knife-fighting. Of course, that is not a failure of MMA since it is, first and foremost, an athletic sport with safety accommodations and rules. However, because the effectiveness and efficiency of MMA makes it suitable for self-defense on the streets, it adapts quite well to the use of and defense against weapons.

A Note About Training

You should aim to train in a martial arts school so that you have live partners to train safely and spar with because training from a book is not enough; you need that "live" energy and resistance that only another person can provide. As you train, focus on results and effectiveness!

CHAPTER 1

Understanding Strategy and Concepts

The crucial foundation for hand-to-hand combat is based on mastering the ranges of fighting, using the natural weapons of your body and knowing where to hit the opponent's body. This is as true for the streets as it is for the ring.

Fighting Ranges

The fighting range describes the distance between you and your opponent. This distance is rarely fixed[1] and changes in the heat of battle. An understanding of fighting ranges requires knowing how to move in and out of range and knowing what offensive and defensive tools work best in the different ranges. Whether you are empty-handed on the streets or wearing gloves in an MMA arena, the following are the four ranges of hand-to-hand combat.[2]

A superior fighter will be able to flow into and out of different fighting ranges at will, and will know the most effective offensive and defensive tools for each range. To fight efficiently, you maximize your strengths and exploit your opponent's weakness. Therefore, against an opponent with excellent boxing skills, a good strategy might be to use a weapon, keep him in kicking range, or close the gap and take him down to the ground.

Kicking / Long Range

In this range, you engage with your opponent primarily with the longest limbs of your body—your legs. This usually favors a tall fighter and an expert kicker like a Muay Thai fighter. A height-disadvantaged fighter will usually try to close the gap to neutralize the kicking range and fight in a closer, more advantageous range.

Kicking / Long Range—The ample space in this range leaves plenty of room for kicking.

Punching / Medium Range

In this range, you engage your opponent primarily with straight punches and wide hooks. You can still kick in this range, but your guard needs to be up because your opponent is close enough to hit you with punches.

Punching / Medium Range—The medium range is conducive to both kicking and punching—so keep your guard up!

---

1   A situation where the range may be fixed is if you're fighting in an elevator.

2   In many martial arts, fighting with a weapon is considered a range in itself. However, a martial artist can fight with a knife in any of the four ranges described here. Remember that an opponent can grab a knife or another weapon when you're fighting in the street.

Trapping / Close Range

In this range, you engage with your opponent primarily with elbows, knees, uppercuts, hooks, grabs, throws, takedowns and headbutts. This is also considered a clinching range, and being able to manipulate your opponent's body and "trap" their limbs will effectively neutralize their hitting capabilities while you remain able to hit them.

Trapping / Close Range—The claustrophobia-inspiring close range brings with it the option of clinching (or being clinched by) your opponent.

Grappling / Extremely Close Range

In this range, you are rolling on the ground attempting to gain a superior position from which to disable your opponent or cause him to submit. The transition into this range is usually initiated by the takedown. Many of the offensive tools you use in the trapping / close range are effective here with the additional offensive tools that are exclusive to the grappling arts such as the arm bar or the triangle choke.

Grappling / Extremely Close Range—Following the takedown, many of the offensive tools that are effective at close range remain so on the ground.

Natural Weapons of the Body

Just about every part of your body can be used as a weapon to strike, pin, leverage or distract your opponent. This is especially true in the clinching and grappling range where tools like shoulder bumps and headbutts are very effective.

1) **HEAD**—to strike with the top or the back of your skull.
2) **TEETH**—for biting, tearing or gnawing on an opponent in an extreme life-or-death situation.
3) **HANDS**—an instinctual and effective tool that can cause a high amount of damage to your opponent. There is a risk of hurting your hand when throwing punches.

    CLOSED HANDS

      Punch—the traditional boxer's weapon used for throwing jabs, crosses, hooks, and uppercuts.

      Hammerfist—a closed fist that hits with the bottom, meaty portion of the hand.

    OPEN HANDS

      Palm—to stun or push an opponent.

      Fingers—to grab, poke, gouge, or pinch an opponent.

      Knifehand—to strike an opponent in certain soft and vulnerable body parts, like the throat.

4) **ELBOWS**—to hit an opponent with the very hard bone in your elbow.
5) **FOREARMS**—used to smash against an opponent's face, throat or other body part.
6) **SHOULDERS**—to bump against your opponent's face in a clinching or grappling situation.
7) **KNEES**—like elbows, these very effective strikes cause high amounts of damage with minimal risk to you.
8) **LEGS**—to strike your opponents with a variety of kicks.
9) **FEET**—to use the instep, heel or ball of your foot in stomping or sweeping your opponent.

You're practically a walking arsenal.

Target Areas of the Body

A key element to finishing a street fight quickly and safely is to target the most vulnerable areas of your opponent's body. Ideally, the best target areas on your opponent's body are those that render him unconscious or prevent him from fighting back. Target areas are best attacked with combination strikes (example: jab to the eyes, kick to the groin, hammerfist to the jaw-line). To improve accuracy with combination strikes, use shadowboxing, cooperative partners and marked punching bags or training dummies.

  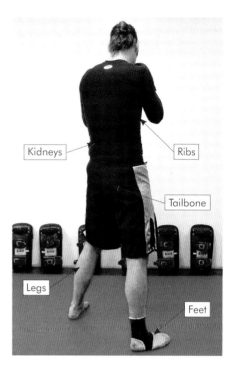

Target these points on your opponent, while you protect your own.

Hand-to-Hand Combat Concepts

A key strategy to adapt from MMA to the streets is to strike quickly and overwhelm your opponent(s) with brutal hits. Clinch if you must, but avoid the ground as much as you can. Strike while in the clinch, and throw or take your opponent down.

When engaging an opponent with strikes in the various ranges (with or without a weapon), you should employ the following critical tactics:

- Neutralize your opponent's offense quickly.
- Emphasize limb destruction.
- Emphasize the angles.
- Emphasize body manipulation.
- Emphasize speed and high hit percentages.

Neutralize Your Opponent's Offense Quickly

Strike before your opponent hits, deceive your opponent or use counterfighting techniques to neutralize your opponent's offense and end the fight quickly. Even in the ring, you don't want to absorb punches like boxer. Although knowing how to "take a punch" is important, the fewer strikes you absorb and the more strikes you give improve your chances for victory (e.g., kicking before an opponent's punch reaches you).

This is a good example of neutralizing the opponent's offense is using a long-range attack: your kick, to stop the opponent's mid-range attack, the cross. Here the kick does damage against the opponent while keeping you at a safe fighting distance out of range of getting hit.

Emphasize Limb Destruction

Focus on hitting an opponent's limbs as well as body and face. Although striking an opponent's limb won't immediately end the fight, it can cause your opponent to lower his guard or feel pain in their limbs (e.g., as with an elbow to an oncoming punch). This can effectively neutralize your opponent's offense.

Here, I am throwing an elbow at my opponent's cross. Done with correct form and proper timing, an elbow thrown at an oncoming punch is a great example of limb destruction. Without healthy limbs (arms, hands, feet and legs), your opponent's ability to fight is rendered nil. Therefore, targeting those areas with counterattacks that break bones or cause great pain (like elbows to punches or foot stomps to feet) will "destroy" your opponent's limbs and end the fight quickly.

Emphasize the Angles

Use angular movement in your footwork to evade and parry incoming strikes and retaliate from a position against which your opponent is unable to defend. Also, hit different areas of your opponent by aiming at high and low targets on the left and right sides. With combination attacks and angular movement, you will be able to: (1) expose different areas of the body to hit, (2) move in and out of ranges, and (3) compound the purpose of your movement with confusing your opponent (e.g., slipping to the outside of an opponent's punch).

This photo shows an example of slipping on the outside of an opponent's punch. A very subtle but effective approach to fighting is to use angular movement. Whether you are moving forward, side-to-side, or retreating, be conscious of your diagonal movements, as well. Diagonal movements allow you to slip punches and to sneak in punches when your opponent is pressing forward. You can either step in diagonal directions or simply move your upper body in diagonal directions to defend or attack.

Emphasize Body Manipulation

Always find ways to control your opponent's body in the clinch or while grappling. By doing so, you keep him unbalanced and vulnerable to your strikes or finishing moves. Also, by manipulating your opponent's body, you can flow into and out of ranges (e.g., getting inside to throw your opponent).

Here, I am positioned to throw my opponent over my shoulder. Learn to manipulate your opponent's body using proper form and leverage so that, once you are in close against your opponent, you can throw him, sweep him, drop him, or lock him quickly and securely.

Emphasize Speed and High Hit Percentages

Speed in striking and movement is important to overwhelm the opponent with a high number of attacks from different angles, and to be able to control the ranges. In addition, aim to overwhelm your opponent with hits until you are sure your opponent is down. For example, many fighters are able to absorb direct hits to the face, so one knee or elbow to the face might not finish the fight. Therefore, you should continue striking with your knees and elbows until your opponent is out. Training that incorporates attacking with combinations is crucial to developing high-hit percentages.

CHAPTER 2

Adopting Proper Stance and Movement

Whether you fight in the ring or on the streets, your stance and your movement are the foundation of your fighting skills. A good stance will allow you to execute your techniques quickly and efficiently in a relaxed, balanced and protected way. Mastering movement for a fight is all about retaining your stance while you're in motion. Whether you're advancing, retreating, moving left or right, striking or defending—you always begin and end in your stance.

Remember: A good stance is your first offense and defense.

The Basic Fighting Stance

The primary purpose of your stance is to be able to hit and defend. A good stance allows you to shift your weight constantly as you move, defend or strike without compromising yourself.

Note the fundamentals for a good fighting stance: relaxed posture, chin tucked, hands up—balanced and ready to spring into action.

The stance begins with your feet, which you should keep a little wider than shoulder-width apart. This helps maintain your body alignment. Always aim to keep your feet under your body as you attempt any move, defense or strike. I like to keep about a 60–40 weight distribution on the balls of my feet. Even though my lead foot is flat on the floor in the picture, in actuality, when I move, I feel most of the weight on the balls of my feet.

The knees are bent to allow for a springy motion and to keep a semi-crouched stance.

Notice that the hands are up and at about eye level. This allows you to protect your face and see your opponent. You can make a loose fist or keep your hands open, as long as you remain relaxed. Your upper body "shield" runs from the tip of your elbows to your fingers.

Carry your head forward with your chin tucked. Your head should feel relaxed. Keep your eye on your opponent and be aware of objects that you can utilize as weapons, additional opponents and escape routes. Keep an eye on your surroundings with your peripheral vision.

Footwork

The whole point of footwork is to advance forward, retreat backward, move left and right or circle around your opponent easily, efficiently and with balance. Aim to develop a rhythmic motion, rocking back and forth and side to side like boxers do.

The following are some strategic footwork concepts:

- **Step and slide forward** to create an opening and force your opponent to strike or move. This allows you to gauge how your opponent reacts to you, which you can use to your strategic advantage.
- **Step and slide backward** to draw your opponent into you or to make your opponent lose their balance as they attack you. Depending on what your opponent does when you move backward, you can determine if they are aggressively attacking or patiently calculating what you're up to.
- **Advance shuffle** to surprise your opponent by closing the distance and defending or attacking aggressively.
- **Retreat shuffle** to escape out of a dire situation when your opponent is overwhelming you with attacks or stepping into you too aggressively.
- **Movement to the left or right** for the same reasons you would when you step and slide forward or backward, except you're moving left or right instead of forward or backward.
- **Quarter-turn to the left or right** to circle away from an opponent's strongest attack and to try to off-balance your opponent.

Note that the instructions for these movements are for a left-foot forward position. If you fight with your right foot forward, then adjust your position as needed.

Step and Slide Forward

Before you run you need to walk, and so, before you can do the advanced shuffle and run circles around your opponent, you need to learn how to step and slide. The step and slide is a formalized way of learning movement and can be used when you want to get in and out of range safely while remaining balanced.

Once you are moving masterfully, you will also be able to make quarter-turns to the left or right around your opponent. Quarter-turns are clock-like movements around your opponent that don't require you to slide. Instead, you pivot yourself in the direction you wish to face your opponent. This is an extremely useful skill to learn for counterfighting.

Begin in your stance.

Distribute your weight to the rear as you take a step forward. Keep your hands up as you move.

Land softly with your lead foot.

Slide the rear foot forward to return to your basic fighting stance. Be sure not to slide your foot so far forward that your stance isn't shoulder-width apart anymore.

Step and Slide Backward

With the step and slide, you can move backward (and left and right) as well. As you get comfortable with the movements, you will integrate them to make them more fluid so that you can easily move in every direction.

Begin in your stance. Distribute your weight to the front as you take a step backward. Keep your hands up as you move.

Land softly with your rear foot.

Slide the lead foot backward to return to your basic fighting stance. As when you're moving forward, be sure not to slide your foot so far backward that your stance isn't shoulder-width apart anymore.

Advance Shuffle

This is basically the step and slide forward with additional speed and constant movement. You will take a sudden, long step forward.

The key here is to develop explosiveness and springiness by keeping your weight mostly on the balls of your feet when you move.

You should do rounds of shadowboxing in which you are just isolating your movement.

Retreat Shuffle

This is basically the step and slide backward with additional speed and constant movement. You will take a sudden, long step backward.

As with the advance shuffle, you should do rounds of shadowboxing in which you are just isolating your movement.

Step and Slide Left

The step and slide left can be used when you want to get into better position for a strike, or dodge an opponent's maneuver.

Begin in your stance.

Distribute your weight to the rear as you take a step to the left with your lead foot. Keep your hands up as you move.

Land softly with your lead foot.

Slide the rear foot to the left to return to your basic fighting stance. Avoid making too wide or too narrow a stance.

Step and Slide Right

Like its leftward counterpart, the step and slide right can be used when you want to get into better position for a strike, or dodge an opponent's maneuver.

Begin in your stance.

Distribute your weight to the lead as you take a step to the right with your rear foot. Keep your hands up as you move.

Land softly with your rear foot.

Slide the lead foot to the right to return to your basic fighting stance. Again, avoid making too wide or too narrow a stance.

Left and Right Shuffle

Same as when you step and slide but done with quick, dynamic movement on the balls of your feet. You will end up taking longer steps, as well.

Quarter-Turn to Your Left

This is a simple move that helps you track a moving opponent while remaining in your stance.

Begin in your stance.

Lean forward as you pivot on your lead foot and swing your rear foot behind you to the right. Keep your hands up as you move.

Complete the turning movement and land softly with your rear foot.

Quarter-Turn to Your Right

Like its leftward counterpart, this is a simple move that helps you track a moving opponent while remaining in your stance.

Begin in your stance.

Lean forward as you pivot on your lead foot and swing your rear foot behind you to the left. Keep your hands up as you move, particularly the lead hand in case your opponent throws a hard strike.

Complete the turning movement and land softly with your rear foot.

Shadow-Boxing

Think about what kind of shadow-boxing you are doing. Are you visualizing a street scenario or a sport-competition scenario? Depending on which, tailor your moves for the particular scenario. For street encounters, aim for explosive, quick and sudden moves. For sport, work your combinations and practice your moves with rounds.

Shadow-box to perfect your fighting skills and put all of your separate techniques together or focus on a specific technique. It's a great warm-up that you can break into rounds so that you can isolate different aspects of your stand-up fighting. For example, you can shadow-box for two minutes by isolating your movement, advancing, retreating and circling around an imaginary opponent. In the next round, you can practice your punches or your kicks or just put it all together as you fight an imaginary opponent.

Shadow-box slowly to improve your form and then speed it up to improve your speed and power. Practice your new techniques by shadowboxing and visualize your defensive and offensive movements against one or more opponents.

CHAPTER 3

Mastering the Upper Body Strikes and Defenses

In this chapter I'll present the fundamentals and purpose of striking for the ring and the street.

Note that these strikes are depicted and written from an orthodox/standard stance where the left hand leads and the left foot faces forward. If you're fighting in an unorthodox stance where your right hand leads and the right foot faces forward, adjust the positions that follow accordingly unless otherwise noted.

Upper Body Strikes

Good fighters are known for their expert hand skills. Most fights may end up on the ground but almost all of them begin standing up. Since fighting on the ground in the streets is something you want to avoid as much as possible, you need to develop proper form, coordination, power, speed and timing with your hand skills.

Jab

In combat sports, the jab is used as a probing tool to determine range, open up the opponent's defense for your attacks and judge an opponent's reaction to your strikes. There are different kinds of jabs: light jab, stiff jab, high and low jab, and double jab. Note that when attempting a low jab as seen in this photo, principles are the same except that you drop your body down by bending at the knee.

Bend at the knees to drop into position to deliver a low jab.

1. Start in a proper and balanced stance.

2. Your strike begins from your lead foot as you pivot, turning your hips and by extension your shoulder. This leads to your arm extending outward.

3. Your arm extends fully straight as if through a point as your foot completes the pivot. Be sure to snap your punch back to your guard in your stance.

Notice from a different angle, I aim not to lift and flare my elbow out so that it does not telegraph my punch.

I fully extend my arm as it strikes and snap it back to my guard when I'm done.

Cross

For many, the cross is the power punch that completes a combination because it requires more body torque and generates more body momentum. It is a very natural, almost intuitive punch to throw. The key to propelling all of the force generated when you turn your body is to keep your body aligned through the movements.

1. Start in a proper and balanced stance.

2. Your strike begins from your rear foot as you pivot, turning your hips and by extension your shoulder. This makes you shift your weight forward.

3. Your arm extends fully straight and straight through a point as your foot completes the pivot. Be sure to snap your punch back to your guard in your stance.

Notice from a different angle, I aim not to lift and flare my elbow out so that it does not telegraph my punch.

I fully extend my arm as it strikes and snap it back to my guard when I'm done.

Note that when attempting a low cross, the principles are the same—except that you drop your body down by bending at the knees.

Bend at the knees to drop into position to deliver a powerful low cross.

Left and Right High Hook

The hook is a short-range weapon with lots of power. It requires precision and timing to pull off effectively. It is best to use it when you're moving into or away from an opponent, especially when your opponent is trying to hit you with a straight punch. Point your palms inward and your knuckles out when you hook.

1. To deliver a solid left hook, start in a proper and balanced stance.

2. Pivot your left foot and turn your left hip and shoulder.

3. With your weight shifted onto your rear foot, complete the hook by driving *through* the mark—not just to the mark. Return back to your defensive guard stance when you're done.

1. To deliver a solid right hook, start in a proper and balanced stance.

2. Pivot your right foot and turn your right hip and shoulder.

3. With your weight shifted onto your lead foot, complete the hook by driving *through* the mark—not just to the mark. Return back to your defensive guard stance when you're done.

Left and Right Body Hook

In principle, the body hooks work exactly with the same leverage and form as the high hooks. The key difference is that you bend at the knees when you throw the hook. Be sure to keep your back straight. Do not lean forward.

1. For the left body hook, start in a proper and balanced stance, then bend at the knees.

2. Pivot your left foot and turn your left hip and shoulder.

3. With your weight shifted onto your rear foot, complete the hook by driving *through* the mark—not just to the mark. Return back to your defensive guard stance when you're done.

1. For the right body hook, start in a proper and balanced stance, then bend at the knees.

2. Pivot your right foot and turn your right hip and shoulder.

3. With your weight shifted onto your lead foot, complete the hook by driving *through* the mark—not just to the mark. Return back to your defensive guard stance when you're done.

Rear Uppercut

The uppercut is another short-range weapon. It is a great punch you can use against fighters who lean forward, as a "surprise" punch or as a counterpunch. Favorite targets are the sternum or under the chin. Note: I'm only demonstrating the rear uppercut, to do a left uppercut, simply do the movements with your left hand.

1. To deliver a solid rear uppercut, start in a proper and balanced stance.

2. Bend at the knees with your back straight. Angle off to the side, just a bit.

3. Come up with your uppercut like a fully-loaded spring. Return back to your defensive guard stance when you're done.

Elbows

Elbows are devastating to use against an opponent because you are striking with the hard bone of your arm. To effectively use the elbow, note the following:

- The elbows are the shortest-range weapon in your arsenal so you must get inside your opponent's guard to deploy it. It is key that you master footwork and defense to allow you to get in close to your opponent at will.
- Be sure to relax the hand of the elbow you are using and tuck it in to make the bone in your elbow flare out as much as possible.
- Use your free hand to protect your face as pictured to avoid getting elbowed in return.

The uncushioned impact of your elbow against an opponent's face can be devastating.

Upper Body Defenses Against Straight Arm Strikes

To be a complete stand-up fighter, you can't just rely on powerful and fast punches; you need good, solid defensive skills. You want to develop a defense that not only protects you from attacks but also sets you up to counterattack.

Outside Parry

The outside parry is a basic and almost instinctual block versus a straight punch. The key is to not overcommit with your parry. You do not need to use too much force when you parry. If you do, your opponent may quickly retract his punch and strike your face in the amount of time it will take you to return your hand to block it. To do the parry, lightly slap the punch coming at you.

To defend against a left hand strike, parry with your right hand.

To defend against a right hand strike, parry with your left hand.

From this angle you can see why a light tap is enough to protect yourself without opening yourself up. In parrying, you only need to clear the area of your face.

Cross Parry

The cross parry is similar to the outside parry but it requires more timing. You also need to angle your upper body a bit to avoid the strike. This is a good way to get inside your opponent's guard and strike with the same hand you parried with. However, be aware that you're also momentarily exposed for the duration of the parry.

To defend against a left hand strike, parry with your left hand by reaching over.

To defend against a right hand strike, parry with your right hand by reaching over.

From this angle you can see how your body has to angle away from the punch. Exploit this movement by stepping inside and striking with a backhand or an elbow.

Inside Parry

This parry is almost like a block. You are using your wrist and forearm to lightly push the punch away. This move also requires excellent timing and you can use this parry to counter a punch and step inside with a punch of your own.

To defend against a left hand strike, parry with your right-hand wrist.

To defend against a right hand strike, parry with your left-hand wrist.

Slip

Slipping is a defensive maneuver that can be used to simply evade straight punches, but when used expertly will give you the benefit of surprise. A slip is an instinctual technique that needs practice and refinement to use efficiently and effectively. An advanced fighter will slip to take advantage of his opponent's opening by getting inside and attacking with punches, traps or takedowns. An advanced fighter learns to slip the left and right straight punches from the outside and the inside.

Slipping to the outside is safer than slipping to the inside because on the outside you avoid both of your opponent's hands. Slipping to the inside requires the same mechanics as slipping to the outside. Practice slipping to the inside with a purpose. When you slip on the inside you need to instantly punch, elbow, knee, clinch, trap or take down because you are vulnerable during that split second.

Against a left-hand strike, slip on the outside by shifting the weight over your lead leg and turning your left shoulder and hip to the right. The punch should barely pass your head to minimize wasted effort.

Against a right-hand strike, slip on the outside by taking a slight step forward and out, angling your shoulder, hip and head to the right.

Shoulder Roll

The shoulder roll is an evasive maneuver away from straight left or right punches. You're rocking backwards and using your elbow to parry the punch or let it ride your triceps. Advanced fighters will attempt to elbow the punch or insert a counter-strike while the opponent is still punching.

Against a right hand strike, lean your weight on the rear foot and allow your hips to rock back. Raise your elbow and tuck your chin into your shoulder. Keep your eye on your opponent.

When viewed from the opposite side, notice that I keep my hand covering my face, my eyes on the opponent and I'm "parrying" his strike with my elbow.

Rock Back

This defensive maneuver is like a last minute evasion when your opponent throws a fast straight punch at you. But it can be used as part of a counterfighting strategy to "crash" into your opponent when your opponent throws the punch and misses your face.

Against a left-handed strike, drop your weight on your rear foot and rock your hips back. As your opponent's punch falls short, return back to your defensive position and strike or keep moving.

The movements are the same for right-handed strike.

Rocking back can also be used against uppercuts and bolo punches. The same principles apply against straight punches, except that the range is shortened in this situation.

Rocking back away from a bolo punch.

Crashing

Crashing is like a forced entry into an opponent's space. It is a very violent and intrusive move when done properly and will give you the upper hand offensively. To perform effectively, you need the element of surprise, good defense and an ability to punch, trap, take-down or throw your opponent. A very fluid way to crash into your opponent is to crash after rocking back from your opponent's strike. Note, however, that with practice and good timing you can crash inside your opponent's hooks, uppercuts, elbows, kicks and even takedown attempts.

1. Rock away from your opponent's strike.

2. It is key to follow your opponent's punch as he returns it to his defensive posture with a quick shuffle or even a "hop" into your opponent's close range. Always keep your hands up, in case your opponent quickly reacts with a strike.

3. Keeping your hands up also allows you to immediately "trap" or "check" your opponent's defense. From here you can do a variety of offensive maneuvers with your hands, arms, legs and feet.

4. Here I opt for an overhand cross into my opponent's jaw line.

5. Here I demonstrate another way to "trap" or "check" your opponent. I use my forearm to block both of his hands using forward pressure. This also frees my other hand up to punch or grab him.

Cover Versus High Hook

The high hook cover is a basic defense that is very easy to do and effective. To perform effectively, it is imperative that you have a solid defensive position to begin with. With this cover, you are opting to absorb the damage with your arms instead of your ears or your head.

The arm comes up close and tight to your head with your elbows down. Cup the back of your head so that your ear is tucked behind your covering wrist or your forearm.

I keep an eye on my opponent and keep my other hand up and ready to defend or attack with it.

The goal is to absorb the punch with the meaty part of your arm and be close enough to counterattack in return.

Cover Versus Low Hook

The low hook cover allows you to cover your torso area without sacrificing your defensive position. The key is to think of your arm from fingertip to elbow as your defensive cover. Again it all begins from the proper defensive position. Once you cover against the low hook shot, bring your hand back up.

The arm drops low, close and tight to the body. Sometimes it helps to lean into the punch to absorb the blow and set yourself up for fighting in your opponent's inside range.

As with the high hook cover, I keep my rear hand up and protecting my face and I keep my eyes on my opponent.

The goal is to absorb the punch with the meaty part of your arm and be close enough to counterattack in return.

Bobbing and Weaving

Bobbing and weaving is an advanced form of slipping, which should be done cautiously and only after much practice. Fighters use it to evade punches while getting inside their opponent's range. You can bob and weave straight punches and hooks, although bobbing against hooks is slightly easier since you have a wider window of time to react. When bobbing straight punches, do it as if you were slipping and duck your head under the punch. Bobbing straight punches can be done inside or outside the punch.

1. Begin in a defensive position. At this point you can bob inside or outside a straight punch or hook.

2. Start by slipping. Note: if you want to get inside your opponent's guard, slip to the outside. If you want to go to the outside of your opponent's guard, slip to the inside.

3. Next drop your head slightly and bend at the knees. Make sure to keep your back straight. Aim to draw the letter "U" with your head as you drop and come back up.

4. As your body comes back up, maintain your guard and counterattack.

1. Here I demonstrate my bobbing and weaving to the outside of an opponent when he hooks.

2. I try to time it as soon as I see my opponent begin his strike. I turn my body slightly inward to help me evade the punch, as well.

3. Note how I don't bend forward and how I drop just enough to let the arm barely pass my head. If you bend forward too much you set yourself up for a knee to the face or a takedown. I also let the punch graze my head so that I don't waste energy avoiding the punch.

4. I quickly pop my head back up on the outside and now my opponent's body is exposed to my attack.

Shoulder Stop

The shoulder stop is a great defense against a hook because you're stopping the strike as soon as it starts. By jamming your opponent, you cause some pain and are able to quickly attack your opponent after the stop. You can do a shoulder stop against a left or right hook or even against a wide cross or haymaker. It's good to follow a shoulder stop with your own hook, elbow or clinch.

This move is done quickly and when you're in medium or close range with your opponent. Using your open palm, ram it into your opponent's shoulder or biceps.

When viewed from a different angle, notice how the shoulder stop throws the opponent off-balance. Play with using a fist instead of an open palm when doing a shoulder stop.

Drop Hand

The drop hand is similar to a parry. You cup your hands and slap the strike before it reaches you. This is used mainly against uppercuts, bolo punches and even front kicks aimed at your chest or chin.

Notice as I use my drop hand against an opponent's left uppercut, I still maintain solid defense.

When viewed from a different angle, notice how I aim to "cup" the punch to ensure accuracy.

Cut the Elbow

Elbows are tricky to defend against because of their close range, sheer brute power and the funky angles they come from. When deployed properly they can cause instant damage. One of the quickest ways to defend against the elbow is to "cut" the elbow strike.

Against an opponent's diagonal elbow, I cut with a knife-hand down as soon as he begins his strike. Aim for the shoulder as if you're trying to chop through it.

Demonstrating against the other side, notice how I immediately grab the back of my opponent's neck to control him before I strike or clinch.

Advanced Upper Body Strikes and Defenses

Once you have a solid foundation with executing your jab, cross, hook, uppercut and elbows, as well as how to defend against them, learning advanced upper body strikes becomes much easier and your arsenal of upper body strikes increases.

Overhand

The overhand is somewhere between the hook and the cross. It's a powerful arched blow that can be used to penetrate basic defensive covers, letting gravity do most of the work. Overhands are not considered "pretty" strikes, especially when used with both hands in a windmill fashion. If done inappropriately, they may also telegraph your strike, which can set you up for your opponent's quick counter.

1. Begin in a defensive guard position.

2. I cock my arm back—but not so much that I'm telegraphing my intent more than necessary.

3. Let gravity do the rest as your fist comes down at your opponent's face.

Overhand Defense: Cover

This is basically a modified high hook cover. The key to doing this correctly against an overhand is recognizing that the overhand is coming at you before it connects, so that you can modify your cover against it.

To cover against my opponent's right overhand, I aim my cover higher to cover more of the top of my head. I aim to "tighten" my cover by touching my forearm and biceps as much as possible. This will make the hole as small as possible, preventing an overhand from barreling through.

Overhand Defense: Shoulder Stop

Another option against an overhand is to step in and shoulder stop it. This must be done aggressively to jam your opponent's momentum. This is a great way to disrupt your opponent, cause him pain and let you follow up with strikes.

Step in and with your open palm, aim for the area right between the shoulder and the biceps.

Bolo Punch

The bolo punch used by many champion boxers lies somewhere between an uppercut and a high hook. It's a devastating angular punch used by fighters to cause damage on the back part of the rib cage.

The bolo punch is somewhere between the body hook and the uppercut. Because it comes in at a funky diagonal angle, it penetrates basic defensive postures. The bolo punch is also used to soften the ribs.

1. Begin in a defensive guard position.

2. I drop my hand as if to do a hook...

3. But then I angle upwards as if to do an uppercut.

4. The bolo punch normally targets your opponent's chest or stomach area.

Bolo Punch Defense: Cover

Covering against a bolo punch requires quick response. It's similar to covering against a body hook but you must be sure to read the opponent's strike so that you can adjust to the diagonal angle from which the bolo punch is coming.

Quickly tuck your elbow in to absorb and deflect the shock of a bolo punch meant for the rib cage.

Backfist

When used effectively, the backfist will surprise your opponent because it's a sudden snap of the fist to your opponent's face. Bruce Lee used it tremendously when he trapped, and MMA fighters could use it effectively if they trained for it more often. The backfist can be done with your left hand or your right hand, solo or in combination with other punches. Here I demonstrate the left backfist.

1. I begin in my defensive guard position.

2. I suddenly cock my arm back. This should be a small and quick movement. Here I am exaggerating for emphasis.

3. Even as I backfist, I keep my other hand up, protecting my face.

4. Complete the strike by hitting the target and then return to your guard position.

Backfist Defense: Cross Parry

You can defend against a backfist similarly to the way you would a straight punch: by parrying, rocking back, and shoulder rolling. Here I demonstrate a cross parry against a backfist.

Cross your hands over to stop the backfist before it connects. From here you can grab the opponent's wrist or crash into your opponent and strike your opponent's exposed ribs on his right side.

Hammerfist

The hammerfist is a vertical strike that can cause damage to the opponent's face, clavicle, shoulders, arms or fists. This strike can also minimize damage to your hand because you're hitting with the meaty part of your fist instead of with your knuckles.

1. I begin in my defensive guard position.

2. I suddenly cock my arm up. This should be a small and quick movement. Here I am exaggerating for emphasis.

3. Come down hard with the strike...

4. Or come down at an angle. Then return to your guard.

Hammerfist Defense: Sheaf

The sheaf is a good defense against the hammerfist because it allows you to stop your opponent's momentum and lets you get inside to counterattack. Here I demonstrate against a right hand hammerfist.

Bring your left arm forcibly up and out. Aim to extend and straighten your left arm so that you can continue attacking your opponent's inside position. It's important that you stiff-arm and step forward as you do this or you risk your opponent's hammerfist crashing through your defense.

Forearm Strike

The forearm strike is another strike that can catch your opponent off-guard when you use it up close, suddenly and violently. The key is to use it when you are inside your opponent's guard and when your opponent's hands are low and not defending properly.

1. Begin in a defensive guard position.

2. I thrust my forearm, aiming for the bridge of my opponent's nose or his throat.

Forearm Defense: Sheaf

To sheaf against the forearm, use a stiff arm and forward momentum.

Bring your right arm forcibly up and out. Aim to extend and straighten your right arm so that you can strike his eyes. It's important that you stiff-arm and step forward as you do this or you risk your opponent's forearm strike crashing through your defense.

From this angle, you can see how my sheaf against his forearm can simultaneously be a finger jab to my opponent's eyes if I continue to straighten my arm as I defend and counter.

Be Prepared to Use "Dirty" Techniques

Dirty techniques are not allowed in the ring or on the mat, but they are easy streetfighting tools to add to your arsenal for encounters outside of the ring that are unpredictable and potentially life-threatening. The great thing about these techniques is that they are easy to work into to your training regimen. They are best used for close-range fighting as a "pain inducer" to set up for follow-up strikes or to control your opponent. Don't be fooled by their simplicity; the reason to train in them is so that when the pressure is on and your heart is pumping, your response will include these techniques. I'm a big believer in the idea that you fight how you train, and if you don't find ways to add these simple tools during your training, you probably won't use them in a fight.

Pinching (Neck, Armpit, Ribs, Thighs)

Pinching requires you to use your fingers like claws that dig deeply into the meaty muscle areas of your opponent. The point is to cause sudden pain and distraction to allow you to finish or control your opponent.

Pinch the *sternocleidomastoid* muscle that runs from the ear to the breastbone. You can also aim for the Adam's apple (not shown).

Grip the *subscapularis* muscle under the arm.

Grip the lower part of the *latissimus dorsi* muscle.

Grip the *adductor* muscle in the inner thigh.

Groin Punching

Punching the groin area is useful when you need to end the fight quickly or escape from certain holds in the street.

Throw a quick low jab or cross to your opponent's groin and immediately return to your fighting stance in case you need to keep attacking.

Hair Pulling

This technique requires your opponent to have long hair—straight or kinky—to be effective. Aim to reach for the side or the back of your opponent's head instead of the top, because it gives you more leverage when you yank and pull.

Reaching from the back, I am able to control my opponent's head and strike with my free hand.

Headbutting

When you want to end the fight quickly and take out your opponent, using your head like a battering ram is the way to go. However, you'd better practice how to do it correctly, or you'll be taking yourself out too!

When you headbutt, make sure to use the top of your head—not your forehead.

Finger Breaking

When your life is on the line, fighting fair goes out the window. Breaking your opponent's finger, like biting, is a last resort option to use against an opponent who has locked you in a hold from which you can't escape.

The photo was taken in this position merely to get a good view of the finger break. Typically, you'll break your opponent's fingers when he has you locked in some kind of restraining hold from which you can't escape, but in which you're able to get a hold of his fingers.

Ear Pulling

It is widely believed that it only takes 7 pounds of pressure to rip a human ear off—a useful fact to know when your life is on the line and you're close enough to reach your opponent's ear.

Here I cup my opponent's ear and place my four fingers behind the ear. Grip and twist. Or pull and rip.

Eye Jab

To do the eye jab effectively, learn how to throw a regular jab and cross to the face. Once you can target the face, then you can develop your precision and accuracy by aiming for the eyes.

Extend your fingertips as if you are making a knife hand and poke at your opponent's eyeball. Return to your fighting stance or follow up with other strikes in combination.

Throat Jab

Same as with the eye jab, master the jab and cross before attempting this attack. Aim below the chin for the throat or Adam's apple.

Extend your fingertips as if you are making a knife hand and stab at your opponent's throat area. Return to your fighting stance or follow up with other strikes in combination.

Raking the Face

We flinch on instinct whenever we get scratched. Raking the face is a savage attack against your opponent where you claw your opponent's face. To make it more effective, dig your claws into your opponent's eyeballs and nose, as well.

Form a claw hand and rake down your opponent's face repeatedly or follow up with other strikes in combination.

Upper Body Combinations

To improve as a fighter, you need to train. The best way to train is in a school where you can practice drills and spar with a variety of opponents. It's also important, when you're training alone, to use shadowboxing and visualization to come up with attack, defense and counter-fighting combinations. String techniques together and test them out. Always keep in mind what your purpose is when you're fighting. Are you fighting in the ring where you're trying to win according to the rules, or are you fighting for survival where you are trying to end the fight quickly? If on the street, do you or your opponent have a weapon? Tailor your fighting to the arena of choice, practice what you learn and come up with your own combinations.

Combination 1:

1. Hook

2. Cross

3. Hook

Combination 2:   1. Backfist   2. Cross   3. Elbow

Combination 3:   1. Hammerfist   2. Body Hook   3. Elbow

Combination 4:   1. Jab   2. Cross   3. Hook

4. Pull Hair   5. Elbow

Combination 5:   1. High Hook   2. Cross to the Groin   3. High Hook

Combination 6:   1. Hammerfist   2. High Hook   3. Pull Hair

4. Hammerfist (setup)   5. Hammerfist (delivery)

Here are a few more combinations to consider:

- Eye or Throat Jab; Elbow; Elbow.
- Forearm to the Face; Bolo Punch; Backfist.
- Cross; Hook; Cross (plus Eye Gouge / Groin Punch).
- Hook; Cross; Hook (plus Hair Pull / Elbow).
- Eye Jab; Cross; Elbow (plus Eye Gouge / Headbutt).
- Overhand; Uppercut; Hammerfist (plus Groin Punch).

CHAPTER 4

Mastering the Lower Body Strikes and Defenses

Like punching, kicking is a natural strike to do during a fight. And like punching, kicking requires proper form and practice to perfect and perform efficiently. The art of kicking has been refined by many different martial arts—particularly Muay Thai, Savate, Sikaran, karate and taekwondo. It is no surprise that amateur and professional mixed martial arts fighters often study under one of the aforementioned arts. It is also easy to adapt kicking for self-defense on the street because you have the additional advantage of wearing shoes, sneakers or boots, adding to the impact of the strike. Be sure to throw these kicks in one swift, confident motion.

Basic Lower Body Strikes

The following basic lower body strikes are very effective in the streets: the roundhouse kicks, front kicks, oblique kicks, foot stomps and knees. Learn to do them with both your lead and rear foot, and in combination.

Rear Roundhouse Kick

The rear roundhouse kick is the "powerhouse" kick. It is usually considered to be the *most* powerful kick because of the distance it travels to the target—it can build lots of momentum before impact.

1. Begin in a defensive guard position.

2. Pivot your lead foot outward as much as possible to allow your hips to "open" up and generate momentum. Raise your rear leg and kick in a downward arch at your opponent's body, ideally below the waist. Note: I am demonstrating a low rear roundhouse kick. The same principles apply if you're aiming above the waist (for middle or upper-body targets) but be aware that it is riskier to strike above the waist than it is to strike below the waist.

3. Aim to kick through your opponent. Try to land your kick using the area from the upper part of your foot to the shin. Keep your hands up and snap your leg back to your defensive position. Note that if you miss the target, immediately return to your defensive position.

Lead Roundhouse Kick

Although not as powerful as the rear roundhouse kick, the lead roundhouse kick can be thrown hard and fast. Many fighters like to begin their striking combinations with the lead roundhouse kick.

1. Begin in a defensive guard position.

2. Pivot your rear foot outward to "open" up your hips and generate momentum. Raise your lead leg and kick in a downward arc at your opponent's body, ideally below the waist. Note: I am demonstrating a low lead roundhouse kick. The same principles apply if you're aiming above the waist (for middle or upper-body targets) but be aware that it is riskier to strike above the waist than it is to strike below the waist.

3. Aim to kick through your opponent. Try to land your kick using the area from the upper part of your foot to the shin. Keep your hands up and snap your leg back to your defensive position. Note that if you miss the target, immediately return to your defensive position.

Lead Front Kick

In Muay Thai, the front kick is also known as a *Tiep*. It is used to knock the wind out of your opponent and to push him back. Because the lead front kick comes up straight forward, it doesn't telegraph your intentions and it doesn't make you lose your balance as much as a roundhouse kick would.

1. Begin in a defensive guard position.

2. Keep your guard up as you raise your lead leg. Raise your lead knee above your waist level.

3. Aim to kick through your opponent. Using the ball of your foot, strike as if you were kicking a door down. Some popular targets are the solar plexus, the stomach, the groin (in a street fight), the thighs or the knees. After kicking, return your foot to the proper defensive position and continue attacking or defending.

Rear Front Kick

Considered a more powerful kick than the lead front kick because of the greater distance it travels to the target (allowing increased momentum to build), this kick is also used to knock the wind out of your opponent and to push him back.

1. Begin in a defensive guard position.

2. Keep your guard up as you raise your rear leg. Raise your rear knee above your waist level.

3. Aim to kick through your opponent. Using the ball of your foot, strike as if you were kicking a door down. Target the same areas as you would with your lead front kick. After kicking, return your foot to the proper defensive position and continue attacking or defending.

Oblique Kick

The oblique kick is found in Savate and Sikaran, among many other arts. It is a short, quick and hard kick that is relatively safe for you to do. It is best done while wearing footwear so that you don't hurt the bottoms of your feet. Kick with the rear foot.

1. Begin in a defensive guard position.

2. Turn your foot outward and "sweep" it forward as if you were kicking a soccer ball.

3. Aim at your opponent's shin or the top of his foot.

Foot Stomp

The Foot Stomp is one of the most common-sense strikes to do against an opponent. It is a safe, quick and brutal strike. You can use the balls of your feet or the heel depending on the stance or position you are in.

1. Begin in a defensive guard position.

2. Raise your rear knee above your waist level.

3. Strike downward with your heel to the top of your opponent's foot.

Lead Knee

The lead knee is a great short-range weapon, best done when you are in the clinch. It can be used as a long-range weapon outside of the clinch but it requires you to have good timing and an understanding of distance to pull it off. Most fighters train to throw multiple knees at an opponent.

1. Begin in a defensive guard position.

2. Raise your lead knee to about waist level and drive your knee forward toward your opponent's midsection or groin.

Rear Knee

Like the lead knee, the rear knee is a great short-range weapon. Not as quickly delivered, it is nonetheless considered a more powerful weapon than the lead knee because of the greater distance it travels to the target (allowing increased momentum to build).

1. The knee can also be timed to catch your opponent when he throws a punch. Against a cross, step outward.

2. Parry the cross with both hands as you thrust your rear knee into your opponent's midsection.

The same parry shown from a different angle.

Roundhouse Kick Defenses

These basic roundhouse kick defenses can be done with either legs or hands (where appropriate), depending on which side your opponent is kicking from. A key point is to avoid using your hands to block kicks below the waist, as this will leave you off balance and susceptible to attack. To perform properly, it requires you to condition your legs to take the impact as well as develop your timing to defend and counter properly.

Shin Block

The shin block is the first defense fighters learn in Muay Thai. Your shins basically absorb the blow coming from an opponent's roundhouse kick. It is usually the first block taught to a fighter because it develops pain tolerance and proper balance.

Defend against a roundhouse kick below the waist by blocking with your shin. This block can be done with either leg depending on which side your opponent is kicking from.

Stump

Another basic defense is "the stump." One performs the stump by absorbing the kicking blow on your thighs. This also develops toughness and pain tolerance in a fighter and allows you to get within range of your opponent so that you can punch and elbow while your opponent kicks.

Defend against an inside roundhouse kick below the waist by blocking with your inner thigh. Turn your thigh inward to meet the impact.

To defend against an outside roundhouse kick below the waist, block with your outer thigh. You can lean forward to meet the impact.

Pass the Kick

After learning the shin block and stump, you can do more advanced defenses against the roundhouse kick like "passing the kick." This move requires excellent timing and agility because you are essentially moving out of the way and parrying the kick at the last possible moment.

In this close-up, I demonstrate the motion necessary to scoop a kick and throw your opponent off-balance.

Against a rear roundhouse kick aimed above the waist, parry the back of the kicking foot.

Cut Kick

Another advanced defense is the "cut kick." With a cut kick, you are kicking your opponent's leg before his kick hits you. This requires quick reflexes and good judgment of distance to do correctly.

Against a roundhouse kick below the waist, kick your opponent's standing leg before his kick lands on you. This is a devastating counter.

Front Kick Defense—Scoop

Scooping the kick is like parrying a punch. The point of the scoop is to redirect the front kick just enough so that it throws your opponent off balance and allows you to evade the kick or enter the opponent's range with takedowns, punches, elbows and knees.

1. Against a front kick aimed above the waist, scoop the bottom of the kicking foot.

2. Scoop and pull the foot toward you to throw your opponent off-balance.

Oblique Kick Defenses

Since the oblique kick is a very deceptive and quick kick, effective defenses against it must be practiced until they are second nature and lightning-fast.

Shuffle Away

Shuffling away might be your only option to avoid the oblique kick. The key is what you do after you shuffle away—get back within fighting range by shuffling back in, or simply escape.

1. Begin in a defensive guard position.

2. As your opponent begins his oblique kick, step back with your rear foot...

3. And slide to move away from your opponent's kick.

Stomp

Once your timing and coordination are improved—or if you are fighting against a slower opponent—you can stomp your opponent's oblique kick. With a stomp, you can damage your opponent's shin, foot or ankle. This also allows you to stay within range so that you can follow up with a combination.

1. Begin in a defensive guard position.

2. Stomp your opponent's leg as he tries to oblique kick you.

Foot Stomp Defense—Shuffle Away

Shuffling away is the easiest way to avoid a foot stomp. Do your best to stay within fighting range so that you can counterattack—unless you simply want to escape from the fight.

1. Begin in a defensive guard position.

2. As your opponent begins his stomp, step back with your rear foot...

3. And slide to move away from your opponent's kick.

Knee Defenses

Since the knees are such devastating weapons, you want to strongly discourage your opponent from using them against you.

Hit the Knee

One of the ways to discourage your opponent from using knees against you is to constantly elbow or knee your opponent's knee every time he uses it against you. To do this correctly requires hours of practice, excellent timing, good judgement and defense-focused sparring with good form.

Horizontal elbow to the knee.

Downward elbow on the knee.

Sudden roundhouse knee against the knee.

Scoop the Knee

This is an advanced move that you can do once you have fine-tuned your accuracy in hitting the knee.

This is a difficult move that requires precision and good timing. As your opponent thrusts his knee, step out and parry-scoop the knee. Use this to off-balance your opponent.

Upper and Lower Body Counterfighting Combinations

Train for the following combinations by shadowboxing, using pads and while sparring. See what works for you while sparring and try to improve what doesn't. Don't be afraid to experiment and come up with your own combinations as well.

Combination 1.

1. Shoulder Roll Opponent's Cross while delivering a Low Lead Kick

2. Cross

3. Hook

Combination 2:

1. Inside Parry Opponent's Cross

(reverse view of Step 1)

2. Jab

(reverse view of Step 2)

3. Hook

4. Cross

Combination 3:

1. Cross Parry Jab

2. Shoulder Roll Cross

3. Shoulder Stop High Hook

4. Elbow

5. Elbow

Combination 4:

1. Cover Overhand

2. Cover Bolo Punch

3. Block Uppercut

4. Cross

Combination 5:

1. Cover Against Hook

2. Hook

3. Backfist (setup)

4. Backfist (delivery)

5. Left Knee

Combination 6:   1. Cover Against Body Hook   2. Uppercut   3. Overhand   4. Elbow (optionally follow-up with a Rear Knee).

Combination 7:   1. Slip Overhand   2. Body Hook   3. Elbow

4. Backfist   5. Overhand   6. Rear Low Kick

Combination 8:   1. Backfist   2. Elbow   3. Knee Groin   4. Foot Stomp

Combination 9:   1. Cut Elbow   (reverse view of Step 1)   2. Elbow

3. Elbow

4. Knee

Combination 10:

1. Outside Parry Jab

2. Slip Cross

3. Left Body Hook

4. Left High Hook

5. Cross

6. Hook

7. Backfist (setup)

8. Backfist (delivery—
optionally follow-up with
a Cross)

Upper and Lower Body Attack Combinations

Be aggressive and accurate when you attack.

Combination 1:

1. Left High Hook

2. Right Cross

3. Left Body Hook

4. Low Rear Kick

Combination 2:   1. Left High Hook   2. Right Cross   3. Left Body Hook   4. Rear Kick

Combination 3:   1. Low Rear Kick   2. Lead Low Kick   3. Hard Cross to the Body   4. Left High Hook

Combination 4:   1. Low Body Jab   2. High Cross   3. Lead Low Kick   4. Rear Knee

Combination 5:   1. Jab   2. Right Uppercut   3. Left Elbow   4. Rear Knee

Combination 6:   1. Jab   2. Right Uppercut   3. Left Hook   4. Rear Low Kick

Combination 7:   1. Lead Low Kick   2. Rear Low Kick   3. Body Hook   4. Cross

Combination 8:   1. Lead Low Kick   2. Front Kick   3. Lead Mid Kick   4. Rear Low Kick

Combination 9:   1. Jab   2. Cross   3. High Hook

4. Backfist (setup)   5. Backfist (delivery)   6. Cross

Combination 10:   1. Rear Mid Kick   2. Lead Knee   3. Cross   Cont.

48

4. Hook and Push

5. Rear Kick (optionally twice)

Combination 11:

1. Lead Low Kick

2. Lead Knee

3. Cross

4. Hook

5. Push

6. Rear Kick (optionally twice)

Combination 12:

1. Oblique Kick

2. Hook

3. Elbow

4. Knee

Combination 13:

1. Cross

2. Hook

CHAPTER 5

Training to Survive a Knife Fight

Fighting hand-to-hand and unarmed is difficult and dangerous enough. Add any type of weapon, whether it is a pen, stick, chain, knife or gun and it becomes exponentially more difficult. The honest truth is that it is best to avoid fighting someone with a weapon—regardless of whether you have a weapon or not—because it is simply too risky. But there are situations that demand that you take the risk: saving or protecting your life or that of someone you love, completing a mission or patrolling a city street. Even though fighting with weapons or against weapons always carries more risk than fighting without them, you have to train in these methods to face the fear and minimize the damage that can ensue. Constant practice builds confidence and develops the calmness you need to keep your cool when facing an escalated life-or-death situation.

Even if your only purpose is to fight in the ring, you should always add weapons fighting to your training. Even though you won't find it in the mainstream sport of mixed martial arts, weapons training fits in with the concept of "mixing martial arts." For one, you can expand on your mixed martial arts foundation and integrate weapons training to many of the skill sets you've already developed. Secondly, it will provide you with an opportunity to train in something different and use your creativity to discover how you would adapt to a dangerous situation. Finally, it can save your life; just being aware of the danger a weapon can pose, let alone how to defend against it, will make you appreciate which techniques you will use to fight in the ring and which techniques you would use to fight in the streets.

Why the Knife?

The scope of this book doesn't permit me to delve into every possible weapon scenario. Furthermore, you need live practice to learn to fight with and defend against weapons. Ideally, these concepts, techniques and drills will be used as a supplement to actual training in a school environment. The reason I chose the knife as the main weapon to focus on is because knives, and knife-like objects such as pens, broken bottles, needles, etc., are everywhere and readily available. Sticks, and stick-like objects like bats, canes, car antennas, etc., are also pretty common but would require more space than I have available here to discuss them properly. The same applies to guns and more exotic weapons, the subjects of which would encompass multiple volumes. Realistically, knives present a more serious problem in that they are readily available, easily concealed and can do very serious, disfiguring damage—if the injuries are survivable. In the following pages you will recognize many concepts and techniques that can also be used with or against sticks and stick-like objects. Nevertheless, the focus of this chapter is on fighting with, and against, an opponent with a single knife.

For safety, make sure you use training knives and goggles when training with weapons.

Grips

The basic common grips to be familiar with are the standard grip and the "ice pick" grip.

The standard grip is preferable for slashing and stabbing while using the "ice pick" grip allows you to conceal the knife and to stab and punch with the knife hand. The standard grip is the most common grip.

The standard grip.

The "ice pick" grip.

General Concepts

When doing stand-up fighting against an opponent with a knife, your main goal is to control the distance by staying out of range of your opponent's attacks. If you're the one holding the knife, you also want to control the distance to prevent counters against you, and do the most damage while minimizing the risk against yourself. While evading the attacks, maintain your defense, keeping your hands up to cover your face. Also, be careful in exposing the inner parts of your wrist and forearms where your veins are located close to the skin. Your other goals against an armed opponent (whether you are armed or not) are to evade and escape or evade and enter (to disarm or finish off your opponent, or otherwise neutralize your opponent). Knife fighting puts your life on the line and can end up with severe legal consequences so always avoid getting into a knife fight as much as possible. During those situations where you *have* to knife fight, do so with intelligence, and integrate streetfighting techniques (like hair pulling, eye gouging, headbutting, etc.) whenever you can.

To be able to evade and counter attacks successfully, you need to understand the different ranges you will fight in, and how to flow in and out of them.

A **long-range** fighting scenario.

A **mid-range** fighting scenario.

A **close-range** fighting scenario.

Continuous Hitting

If you're fighting for your life and you're in a kill-or-be-killed situation, then you must attack non-stop until your opponent drops before you. Otherwise, his adrenaline will outlast the first attack and he will still come at you. There have been many cases of knife attacks where the victim didn't even realize they were cut and bleeding until after the fight was over.

Strike the Best Target First

Hit the best target before your opponent hits you. This is pretty straightforward target selection. Aim for targets that will cause immediate pain or make your opponent flinch. This is why, for example, I emphasize hitting the eyes and the groin over punching the stomach in life-or-death situations.

Stance and Protection

Similar to the unarmed defensive stance, keep your guard up and hold the knife in your lead hand to be able to slash and stab quickly. Some knife fighters advocate holding the knife in the rear hand to secure and hide the weapon better but the advantage of having the knife in the lead hand is that it puts it closer to the enemy target and will appear to be more intimidating. Be sure to keep the knife in motion with figure eight movements but don't make the movements too large. Be quick to slash and stab when your opponent attacks.

Demonstrations of a good fighting stance with the knife: hand covering my face, knife hand up, chin down, and weight balanced comfortably on my feet.

What we wear factors into how protected we are if we fight an armed opponent. We can't always determine where we fight so it's possible to be attacked when we are at the beach or in a location where we are least clothed. Soldiers and cops have the option of wearing layers and body armor because they anticipate the situation. But even soldiers and cops aren't always wearing their armored uniforms. As civilians, we can strike a balance between the clothes we wear for fashion and the clothes we wear for protection. Consider wearing slash-proof or puncture-resistant gloves in place of regular leather gloves. Weather permitting, wearing layered or thick clothing will also help. Technology and fashion are merging and jackets, shirts and pants are also being made that are slash-proof or puncture resistant. Finally, depending on which state you live in, you may be allowed to carry weapons. If you are given that privilege, be sensible. Get the proper training in using the weapon and treat the weapon with the seriousness it deserves. Be confident, but don't be cocky just because you are armed. It's not the weapon that is dangerous but the person who is using it.

Basic Strikes (Slashing and Thrusting)

Knife strikes and thrusts are based on forward and angular movement. When slashing or thrusting with a knife, your rear hand should be up protecting your face. This rear hand is known as the "live" hand, which you can use to throw punches or grab your opponent when the opportunity arises.

Diagonal Attack

Attack in a slashing "X" fashion from top to bottom, starting from the right.

The diagonal slash.

Horizontal Attack

Attack the middle area from right to left.

The horizontal slash.

Thrust

Thrust forward toward the middle area.

A basic knife thrust.

You can also thrust high and low.

A high thrust.   A low thrust.

Unarmed Tactics Against a Knife-Wielding Foe

If you find yourself fighting an opponent with a knife and you are unarmed, you are obviously already at an immediate disadvantage. Even trained fighters are at risk to lose their life or limb against an opponent with a knife. It's not impossible to defeat an armed opponent if you are unarmed but it can be a difficult, bloody mess. The following sections give an overview of your options.

Run

If you have to fight an armed opponent, there is no shame in running away if you can, providing that it won't expose you or a loved one to more danger. As professional fighters and disciplined martial artists, we are expected to develop and have judgment about which fights are worth taking up and which risks are worth taking. Fighting an armed opponent to protect yourself when you're cornered or protect someone you love is worth the risk. Otherwise, use your legs to run.

Shield

If you have to fight unarmed, keep your hands up and protect the inner parts of your forearms and wrist. Hopefully, you're wearing a thick leather jacket that might be able to protect you from some slashes. If not, look for some type of thick fabric or material you can wrap around your arms. You can also use large objects, like a chair, to keep your opponent's knife away and find room to run.

Wrapping a towel around your arm might provide some limited temporary protection, which can give you the opportunity to get inside and fight back or to run away.

Dodge

It's an obvious reaction to keep your distance from an armed opponent. The important thing to remember when you are dodging is that your movements should help you achieve your final goal—whether it is to run away or to counter attack. If you are dodging to run away then you have to pay attention to whatever exits are available, how many people are with you or against you in the situation, and what objects you can use to shield yourself, all while keeping your distance from the knife. Your main goal is to move away so that you can be in the best position to escape freely. If you are trying to counterattack then not only are you focusing on the people and objects around you, but you are also trying to find the right moment to launch your counterattack.

Move back and away from diagonal, horizontal and thrusting strikes.

Many will say that dodging is common sense, so why train to move away? The point is that this is how you start to develop your reflexes and your understanding of timing and distance so that you can intercept, block and strike a knife-wielding opponent if you're ever in that situation.

Interception

Interception is striking before the opponent hits you. Once the knife is out and you feel that your life is in danger, don't hesitate to attack if you can. Even if you don't plan on going all the way and taking down your opponent, an intercepting strike will give you a window of opportunity to run away and get help or get your loved ones out of a dangerous situation. The key to a successful interception is speed. Aim for an opponent's vulnerable points like the eyes, the throat, or the genitals. You can also use a distracting strike like the oblique kick to set up your attack to a vulnerable spot.

Evasive Angling

It's hard to notice because of their inability to portray depth, but in these pictures I am angling to one side or another to be able to avoid the knife. Avoid being in the direct line of the knife as much as possible.

Eye jab—angle left, and stiffen your fingers and jab the eyes.

Groin kick—angle right, and place a swift kick to the groin.

Oblique kick—angle right, and kick the shin or the knee.

Block and Jab

Block the knife strike with your forearm and jab with your other hand. Aim for vulnerable spots like the eyes or the throat. The following are basic blocks and jabs against an opponent holding a knife in either a standard or ice pick grip. Blocking and jabbing gives you a better chance of survival than doing nothing against an opponent but you need to be prepared for the strong possibility that you will get cut. Your blocks and jabs should minimize the possibility—especially if you've shielded or covered your blocking hand—but you need to mentally prepare for that eventuality and fight through it so that you can survive.

The following are various block and jab strategic scenarios.

Block and eye jab against a diagonal strike from your opponent's right.

1. Time the block.

2. Stiff block and attack the eyes at the same time.

Block and eye jab against a diagonal strike from your opponent's left.

1. Time the block.

2. Stiff block and attack the eyes at the same time.

Block and eye jab against a horizontal strike from your opponent's right.

1. Time the block.

2. Stiff block and attack the eyes at the same time.

Block and eye jab against a horizontal strike from your opponent's left.

1. Time the block against the sweeping strike coming from the left.

2. Stiff block and attack the eyes at the same time.

Block and eye jab against a thrust strike.

1. Because the attack is coming straight forward, you need to angle out just enough so that you can evade the strike while still being able to block the thrust and attack the eyes.

2. Stiff block and attack the eyes at the same time.

Block and eye jab against a downward strike.

1. Time the block.

2. Stiff block and attack the eyes at the same time.

Block and eye jab against a downward strike (ice pick grip).

1. This block is very risky to perform, so your timing must be on point.

2. Stiff block and attack the eyes at the same time.

Advanced Blocks and Strikes

Once you've cultivated the timing and confidence to block and eye jab, you can practice more advanced techniques like adding additional strikes, grabbing the weapon and disarming your opponent. As I've said before, knife fights are nasty and are best avoided. If you must fight then you want it to be short and provide you an opportunity to escape. Trying to strip the knife or getting into a long knife fight should be the last thing in your mind. They should only be attempted if there is no clear avenue for escape or an opportunity presents itself. Remember: your opponent holding the knife is determined to cut or kill you so he or she will not let go of the knife willingly.

The following are some key points to remember when you are trying to disarm and disable a knife fighter:

- Cause severe pain by striking the eyes, the throat and other sensitive areas.
- Control your opponent's weapon hand.
- Mentally steel yourself to fight on even if you get cut.
- If you can't completely disarm, then redirect the opponent's knife into their body.
- Be aggressive.

Stripping the Knife

Stripping the knife is a knife-disarming technique that allows you to keep the knife in your hand once you disarm your opponent.

1. Stripping the knife is one way to disarm your opponent. It is a very delicate maneuver that requires precision, leverage and violence of action. Grab the opponent's knife hand, gripping the meaty part of his thumb and twist his hand at the wrist to cause pain.

2. Keeping your opponent's wrist hand twisted, aim for the hilt part of the knife (away from the sharp edge) and push it against his thumb.

3. Strip the knife from his hand and keep it so that you can attack him. Continue twisting his hand.

Defending Against Knife Strikes

To defend against a diagonal strike from your opponent's right, follow these steps.

1. Block and eye jab.

2. Kick the groin.

3. Your opponent should be disoriented. If he still hasn't dropped the knife, scoop it downward and away so that you can gain control of the knife.

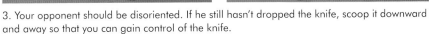

4. Strip the knife (refer to the close-ups on page 57 for hand placement).

5. Attack your opponent.

To defend against a diagonal strike from your opponent's left, follow these steps.

1. Block and eye jab.

2. Oblique kick your opponent's shin, knee, or the top of his foot.

3. While your opponent is disoriented, grab the meaty part of his knife hand.

4. Strip the knife (refer to the close-ups on page 57 for hand placement).

5. Attack your opponent.

To defend against a horizontal strike from your opponent's right, follow these steps.

1. Block and eye jab.

2. Vertical elbow to the opponent's throat or elbow smash your opponent's face.

3. While your opponent is disoriented, scoop his knife hand downward and away so that you can gain control of the knife. Grab the meaty part of his hand.

4. Strip the knife (refer to the close-ups on the top of page 57 for hand placement).

5. Attack your opponent.

To defend against a horizontal strike from your opponent's left, follow these steps.

1. Block and eye jab.

2. Stomp the top of your opponent's foot.

3. While your opponent is disoriented, grab the meaty part of his hand.

4. Strip the knife (refer to the close-ups on the top of page 57 for hand placement).

5. Attack your opponent.

To defend against a thrust strike, follow these steps.

1. Block and eye jab.

2. Knee your opponent's thigh.

3. While your opponent is disoriented, grab the meaty part of his hand.

4. Strip the knife (refer to the close-ups on the top of page 57 for hand placement).

5. Attack your opponent.

To defend against a downward strike (ice pick grip), follow these steps.

1. Time your movement and evade the strike, parrying your opponent's knife hand.

2. Continue the parry so that your opponent stabs his own leg and follow with an eye jab.

3. If your opponent still has the knife, bring it up and out, gripping the meat part of his palm. Be sure to make his wrist turn so that the knife is almost pointing at him.

4. While still gripping his hand, grab the knife.

5. Attack your opponent.

Weapons of Opportunity

As a martial artist you are trained to become a weapon. You also learn to use objects that aren't meant to be weapons as weapons. When you find yourself facing an armed attacker, assess your environment to find "weapons of opportunity" that can even the odds for you a bit—it could be a car antenna, a desk lamp, a textbook, a beer bottle, a rock, etc. As long as it protects you and allows you to equalize the situation, use it. Use your creativity and imagination to invest some training time using non-weapons as weapons, and scan the places you frequent for possible weapons that you can use in the case of an emergency.

Knife Versus Knife—Striking with Your Weapon

Fighting with a knife is very instinctual but it needs to be trained for properly so that you can retain your weapon and inflict the most amount of damage in the shortest amount of time—with minimal injury to yourself. Training with a knife requires constant practice and supervision. Within the scope of this book, I will cover the basic concepts.

"Defang the Snake" Versus Knife Attacks

"Defanging the snake" is a simple Filipino kali concept which suggests that a snake with no fangs is a harmless snake. Therefore, in a knife fight, unless a prime target like the face is clearly open and you can strike without getting hurt, you should strike at your opponent's knife hand instead. Cutting your opponent's knife hand essentially disarms your opponent because he is now cut and bleeding and you are still armed and safe.

The following are various strategic knife hand strike scenarios.

Knife hand strike against a diagonal strike from your opponent's right.

Quickly slash diagonally before your opponent reaches you.

Knife hand strike against a diagonal strike from your opponent's left.

Quickly slash diagonally before your opponent reaches you and move your body away from the oncoming slash.

Knife hand strike against a horizontal strike from your opponent's right.

Quickly slash diagonally before your opponent reaches you.

Knife hand strike against a horizontal strike from your opponent's left.

Quickly slash diagonally before your opponent reaches you and move your body away from the oncoming slash.

Knife hand strike against a thrust strike.

Quickly slash diagonally before your opponent reaches you and move your body away from the oncoming slash.

Knife hand strike against a downward strike.

Quickly slash and escape.

Knife hand strike against a downward strike (ice pick grip).

Quickly slash and escape.

Block and Stab Versus Knife Attacks

Just as when you are unarmed, you can block and attack with a knife. The concepts remain the same except that you are attacking with your knife instead of an eye jab and you are using your free hand to check and parry your opponent's knife hand.

The following are various strategic block and stab scenarios.

Block and stab against a diagonal strike from your opponent's right.

The block and stab has to occur nearly simultaneously; block your opponent's knife a split second before you stab.

Block and stab against a diagonal strike from your opponent's left.

Note that here you must check and parry with your free hand, unlike when you were unarmed.

Block and stab against a horizontal strike from your opponent's right.

The block and stab has to occur nearly simultaneously; block your opponent's knife a split second before you stab.

Block and stab against a horizontal strike from your opponent's left.

Note that here you must check and parry with your free hand, unlike when you were unarmed.

Block and stab against a thrust strike.

Note that here you must check and parry with your free hand, unlike when you were unarmed.

Block and stab against a downward strike (your opponent is holding the knife in an ice pick grip).

Note that here you must check and parry with your free hand, unlike when you were unarmed.

CHAPTER 6

Owning the Clinch

The clinching range falls somewhere between the punching and grappling range. In fact, many call it "stand-up" grappling. Most fighters do not like to fight in this range and prefer either punching and kicking or going all the way and taking it to the ground. However, the clinching range rewards those who have mastered how to fight within that distance. In the clinch, you can defeat many of those very fighters who prefer to take it to the ground or to punch and kick with distance between them. Boxers and Thai fighters use the clinch not just to catch their breath, but to punish their opponent with devastating up-close strikes to the face, midsection and legs. A master clinch fighter can control his opponent, almost at will, in this range and end the fight very quickly. A modern fighter, whether he fights in the ring or defends himself in the street, needs to master the basics of how to clinch and how to defend and attack in the clinch.

Basic Clinch Positions and Holds

The most common and effective clinching holds come from Muay Thai, Western boxing and wrestling. There are many variations and holds to learn and master, but the three basic ones with which a good fighter should be comfortable are: the Muay Thai clinch, the double hand wrap, and the single neck grip.

Muay Thai Clinch

The Muay Thai clinch is one of the most effective and tested techniques in the world. It is a powerful weapon to use at close range because it allows you to control your opponent's movement while you knee and kick with impunity.

Grab the back of your opponent's neck and lean against him with your forearms on his chest. Your clasp should be so tight that your elbows can almost touch each other and you should squeeze his neck with your forearms. Do not interlace your fingers; instead place one hand over the other to grab the back of his neck.

1. Reach over your opponent's arms and clasp your hands underneath them. Do not interlace your fingers.

2. You can unclasp your hands briefly to push your opponent back so that you can attack him, or to block your opponent's knee strike.

Double Hand Wrap

Used strategically by boxers, grapplers and wrestlers, the double hand wrap is another weapon that allows you to neutralize your opponent's offensive capabilities while attacking him.

Single Neck Grip

A combination and modification of the Muay Thai clinch and the double hand wrap, this clinch allows you to both control your opponent and neutralize his offensive capabilities. Even though you are partially exposed, a master clincher will defend by moving his opponent (via the neck control) and then attacking him in the vulnerable areas.

Grab wrist and neck.   Grab elbow and neck.   Grab elbow and neck on the same line.   Grab arm and neck.

Defense Against the Clinch Attempt

The easiest way to defend against the clinch is to prevent being put into the clinch in the first place. Of course, that is easier said than done. A main point to remember if you're in a Muay Thai clinch or a single neck grip: keep your head and neck stiff and straight to reduce your opponent's ability to control you in the clinch or knee you in the face. The next thing to consider when attempting to escape any clinch is to find an opening and exploit it. Escaping the double hand wrap and the single neck grip is simpler than escaping the Muay Thai clinch because you are only partially under your opponent's control. Thus, one of the simplest ways to escape the double hand wrap and the single neck grip is to wait for your opponent to make his move and use that opening to your advantage. Your options are to do one of the following:

- Escape the clinch and put your opponent in the clinch;
- Defend and fight within the clinch;
- Escape the clinch and fight from a distance, or;
- Escape the clinch and get away.

The last two options are best if you don't feel comfortable in the clinching range and prefer the distance to take advantage of a weapon, use your kicks and punches or to simply get away. My preferred option is to regain the clinch and use it to my advantage with my attacks within the clinch. The following defenses are against the Muay Thai clinch where the opponent has a firmer grip and control against you and can hurt you more readily.

Clinch Escape and Reversal

You should try your best to avoid being put in the clinch, but it's inevitable that you will find yourself in one at some point. If put in the clinch: you should immediately react by escaping the clinch before your opponent gets a solid grip on you. From there take advantage of the close range and put your opponent in the clinch.

Turn Shoulders In to Regain Control

To escape a Muay Thai clinch, you first have to remove the area of leverage your opponent is using against you to manipulate your body. Because your opponent is pressing down on your shoulders to grip your neck, you need to adjust your shoulders so that your opponent can no longer grip you effectively. To do this, turn your shoulders in.

1. Your opponent has you in their clinch. Turn your shoulder inside (in this case, I chose my right shoulder).

2. Clasp the back of your opponent's head.

3. Turn your other shoulder in.

4. Clinch your opponent and immediately move him or attack him.

Push Opponent's Clinching Elbow Up

Sometimes your opponent has you gripped so strongly that you can't turn your shoulders in. Another way to escape is to push up on your opponent's elbows until his arms are over your head.

1. Your opponent has you in their clinch.

2. Push your opponent's arms up off of your neck.

3. Immediately grab your opponent and grab his neck and arm on the same line.

Cross Parry Opponent's Clinching Elbow

A more advanced way to escape the clinch allows you to lock your opponent's arm to keep him vulnerable to your attack. The key here is to push up on one of your opponent's arms and "lock" it against his other arm. Once you have him "locked" in a modified clinching position, you can attack him with knees and punches.

1. Your opponent has you in their clinch.

2. Push one of his arms up (in this case, I chose his right arm).

3. Put the arm you pushed up over his other arm that is still gripping your neck (this will lock his arms). Reach over and grab the back of his neck.

4. Put opponent in a Muay Thai clinch while his arms are locked.

Elbow Down on Opponent's Clinch Grip

If you can't push up on your opponent's elbows, then use your elbows to strike downward on your opponent's clinching arms. You will need to turn your shoulders in somewhat so that you can generate the leverage and momentum you need to break your opponent's clinching grip.

1. Your opponent has you in their clinch.

2. Raise one of your arms up and elbow down on your opponent's arm (in this case, I chose my left elbow).

3. As soon as his arm drops, reach and grab the back of your opponent's neck. From here you can elbow down on the other arm, the same way, and put him in a Muay Thai clinch.

Defending and Fighting Within the Clinch

Many times your opponent will end up with a solid grip on you because he caught you by surprise, was too quick and strong, or you were too tired. From there, your opponent will surely attack you so you will be forced to defend against the attacks. Although it is not the ideal position to be in, you can still fight back inside your opponent's clinch.

Covering Versus Body Hooks, Knees and Elbows

Whenever you are in the clinch, expect your opponent to use upper and lower body strikes and takedowns against you. You will need to develop a "6th sense" in defending yourself against strikes and elbows while you're being held. The only ways to develop this "6th sense" is through live partner training and clinch sparring.

To throw a body hook, your opponent will have to disengage from the clinch temporarily. Cover against the body hook and look for an opening to counter.

Punish your opponent's legs by elbowing his knees when he knees you. Be sure to avoid bending forward too much so that your opponent doesn't end up kneeing you in the face. Straighten back up, stiffen your neck and find a way to escape or counter once he stops kneeing you.

To throw an elbow, your opponent will have to disengage from the clinch temporarily. Block your opponent's elbow by "cutting" it before he fully throws it. Use this as an opportunity to counter the clinch and put him in yours.

Hitting Back

One drawback for the clincher is that his midsection is exposed while he has his opponent in the clinch. If he hasn't trained how to attack and defend aggressively and decisively in the clinch, he will be vulnerable in this position.

Throw body hooks.

Turn your shoulder in and throw a vertical elbow.

Lean back for a short-range knee to his thigh (street fight: knee the groin).

Fighting While Applying the Clinch

The clinch is ideal to control your opponent. Controlling your opponent means you move your opponent in all directions to aggravate him, wear him down and place him in a position vulnerable to your attacks. Your attacks in the clinch have to be aggressive, intuitive, precise and fast because you will be briefly vulnerable and your opponent will try to escape.

Hitting with Arms

When you strike with your arms, immediately put your opponent back in your clinching grips as soon as you're done striking.

Body hook: begin in the clinch. Disengage with one hand to deliver a body hook while keeping your opponent gripped with your other hand. Return immediately to your clinch.

Uppercut: begin in the clinch. Disengage with one hand to deliver an uppercut while keeping your opponent gripped with your other hand.

Elbows: begin in the clinch. Disengage with one hand to deliver an elbow while keeping your opponent gripped with your other hand.

Hitting with Legs

The clinch is best used with added leg strikes like stomps and knees because you can fully control and attack in unison.

Foot stomps: begin in the clinch. While in the clinch, move your opponent and deliver a foot stomp.

Knees: begin in the clinch. While in the clinch, move your opponent and deliver a knee.

Streetfighting Strikes In the Clinch

Headbutting

Maintain your grip on your opponent's head, bend at the knees and thrust the top of your head to the bridge of your opponent's nose.

Headbutting illustrated.

Raking the Face

Raking the face is a gruesome technique to use when your life is on the line and you want to aggravate your opponent and cause enough pain to allow you to finish him off with your finishing moves.

Raking the face.

Eye Gouging

Eye gouging is another gruesome technique to use when your life is on the line.

1. Gouge your opponent's eyes.

2. For devastating results, follow up with the headbutt, knee to the groin and elbow, as well.

Hair Pulling

This is an obvious but often forgotten technique to use against an opponent to cause pain and set him up for your finishing strikes. You can also pull your opponent's ear, in case they have very short hair, are bald, or have their hair covered.

Grab your opponent's hair to cause pain and move his head into position for a strike.

Knee to the Groin

While controlling your opponent in the clinch in a streetfight, throw consecutive strikes to your opponent's groin area with either knee.

The disabling pain from a knee to the groin will allow you to escape or set up finishing strikes.

Getting In and Out of the Clinch

It is critical to know how to safely enter into the clinching range in a fight, to catch your opponent by surprise and to be able to pull off your finishing moves effectively.

Neck Wrestling I

This is a good warm-up exercise to do back and forth with a training partner to get used to getting in and out of the clinch. Both partners should take turns performing the moves I am demonstrating. Aim for a rhythmic flow, you and your partner should give some resistance, but only at about 70%—so that you're not fighting too hard and can concentrate on a good flowing movement.

1. Opponent has you in his clinch.

2. Turn your shoulder in (for demonstration, I used my right side).

3. Grab your opponent's neck.

4. Bring your other arm through the middle gap. This helps to break your opponent's grip.

5. Now you have your opponent in your clinch. He will then proceed to do what you just did. Continue back and forth.

Neck Wrestling II (Wrapping Opponent's Single Arm or Both Arms)

This is a variation of the neck wrestling warm-up exercise that you can do back and forth with a training partner to get used to getting in and out of the clinch. Here, instead of going for the Muay Thai clinch, you will wrap one or both arms. Both partners should take turns performing the moves I am demonstrating. Here, I am demonstrating wrapping one arm but you can mirror the moves and wrap the other arm instead of going for the neck. Also, instead of wrapping around the arm, you can grab the wrist or the triceps. Again, aim for a rhythmic flow, where you and your partners should give about 70% resistance.

1. Opponent has you in his clinch.

2. Turn your shoulder in (for demonstration, I used my right side).

3. Grab your opponent's neck.

4. Bring your other arm through the middle gap. This helps to break your opponent's grip.

5. Wrap around the arm and maintain a solid grip on the neck.

Attacking Before Opponent Attacks

Many fighters don't feel comfortable in the clinching range because they feel vulnerable or don't have the necessary timing or techniques to survive within that range. They prefer to keep the fight in the punching or kicking range or even take it to the ground than to stand there and clinch. This is why a master clincher can do damage in a fight by taking advantage of this underused range. If you feel confident in your clinching skills and have good timing, you can attack and clinch before your opponent can attack you.

The following are some combinations you can do in the street.

Attack and Clinch In the Street I

This combination is effective to neutralize your opponent's leg with a good oblique kick to the opponent's shin or knee. Although the series here ends with a Muay Thai clinch, you can continue striking your opponent while keeping him in the clinch with upper and lower body strikes or simply drop him with a throw or a takedown.

1. Face your opponent in a good defensive stance.

2. Oblique kick your opponent's shin, knee or foot.

3. Throw a hook.

4. Follow up with an elbow.

5. Thrust a hard rear knee into your opponent.

6. Wrap your arms around your opponent's head and put him in a Muay Thai clinch. From here you can follow with more attacks or move him into a more vulnerable position.

Attack and Clinch In the Street II

This combination is a quicker and much more brutal fight-finisher.

1. Face your opponent in a good defensive stance.

2. Get the jump on your opponent and slap down his hands to prevent him from blocking your attack.

3. As you slide your hands up to clinch him, gouge his eyes.

4. As you're about to put your opponent in your Muay Thai clinch, grab and pull his hair to the side.

5. Headbutt your opponent and keep him in your clinch.

Counterfighting Your Opponent's Attacks with the Clinch

One good way to get inside and clinch against your opponent is to do it when he throws a strike at you. You can use your timing and aggressiveness to get inside while your opponent is momentarily vulnerable. In fact, once you've honed your skills, clinching your opponent as a counterfighting strategy is recommended whenever he attacks. This can wear him down—physically and psychologically—as well as open him up to your finishing moves. However, you need to have a good, solid defense and attuned reaction senses to be able to get inside safely.

The following are some combinations you can do as part of your counterfighting and clinching strategy for the ring or the street.

Counterfighting and the Clinch I

One of my favorite ways of clinching my opponent is when I am counterattacking. This technique relies on taking advantage of your opponent's temporary moment of vulnerability when he is punching. It is important to train your speed, timing and accuracy to do moves like this effectively.

1. Face your opponent in a good defensive stance.

2. Your opponent throws a hook and you cover the hook.

3. Immediately wrap around your opponent's hooking arm.

4. Grab around your opponent's neck with your other arm.

5. Thrust a hard rear knee into your opponent.

Counterfighting and the Clinch II

Here is another one of my favored clinching methods.

1. Face your opponent in a good defensive stance.

2. Your opponent throws a jab and you block it with an inside parry.

3. Immediately follow up your inside parry by throwing a cross with the same hand.

4. Follow up with an elbow.

5. Thrust your forearm into your opponent.

6. Wrap your arms around your opponent's neck and put him in a Muay Thai clinch. From here you can follow with more attacks or move him into a more vulnerable position.

Counterfighting and the Clinch III

Here is a good clinching method to use after you parry your opponent's cross.

1. Face your opponent in a good defensive stance.

2. Your opponent throws a cross, so you use an outside parry to cover while dropping your rear arm and bringing it up in the inside line of your opponent's body.

3. Form a vertical elbow with the arm you initially dropped and strike your opponent's face with it.

4. With your opponent's arm locked on top of your shoulder, wrap the arm you used to elbow your opponent around his neck putting him in a single neck grip clinch. From here you can follow with more attacks or move him into a more vulnerable position.

Counterfighting and the Clinch IV

Another way to put your opponent in a good clinch is to do so after softening him up with your strikes. After blocking his attack and following up with yours, your opponent will be "dazed and confused" and less able to fight back against your clinch.

1. Face your opponent in a good defensive stance.

2. Your opponent throws a rear low-line kick, which you block with your shin.

3. Drop your foot and immediately follow up with a lead leg low-line kick to your opponent's inner thigh.

4. Follow up with a rear cross.

5. Then throw a high hook.

6. With the hand you used to throw the high hook, grab your opponent's neck and put him in a Muay Thai clinch. From here you can follow with more attacks or move him into a more vulnerable position.

Clinch Fighting with the Knife

As dangerous as it is to fight in the clinch, fighting an opponent with a knife in the clinch is even more so. In this situation, it is much harder to escape because your opponent has you in his grips and the surprise factor increases since a knife can be pulled out mid-fight and used against you in a heartbeat. Still, learning to defend yourself requires you to train for situations like this so that you can minimize the potential damage and disarm your opponent. To succeed in this range, your reaction timing and your intuitive senses must be trained to a heightened degree. It requires hours and months of constant practice to develop the necessary attributes.

Basic Principles of Fighting Unarmed Against an Armed Opponent

If your opponent has successfully clinched you with a solid grip on your neck or around your arm and he has a knife, he will proceed to slash and thrust with his knife from high and low, horizontal and diagonal angles. He will aim to maintain control on your neck or arm while he strikes quickly and violently.

When caught in that situation, your goal is to block the knife or evade the knife while simultaneously attacking your opponent. You need to create some space within that range so that you can defend and attack, and have time to react. You will then follow with attempts to disarm or use the knife against your opponent. Use these defenses or evasions depending on the approaching angle of the attacker's knife.

Block: while being held in a single neck grip, your opponent tries to slash you with his knife. Jab your opponent's eye with one hand while blocking the knife with the other. While your opponent is in pain, take the opportunity to escape, strip the knife, or continue hitting.

Shoulder stop block: while being held in a single neck grip, your opponent tries to thrust his knife at you. Jam your palm hard into your opponent's shoulder or biceps. While your opponent is in pain, take the opportunity to escape, strip the knife, or continue hitting.

Scoop: if your opponent tries to slash you low, place your hand palm up and "scoop" the knife hand past you. Once you have defended against the low slash you must escape, strip the knife, or begin to hit your opponent in vulnerable target areas.

Parry pass: while being held in a single neck grip, your opponent tries to thrust low with his knife. Angle your body by stepping out to avoid the thrust while parrying with your hand. Almost simultaneously with the parry pass, jab your opponent's eyes. While your opponent is in pain, take the opportunity to escape, strip the knife, or continue hitting.

The following are additional attacks that will distract and cause your opponent pain. These attacks can be done before the knife attack or after the knife attack. It is recommended to continue using a variety of attacks in combination until you are able to escape, or your opponent is neutralized or disarmed.

Knee: if you have escaped your opponent's clinch but he is still attacking with his knife, parry and hold the knife hand while you thrust a knee.

Elbow: if you are able to loosen your opponent's single neck grip as he tries a low slash, you can insert an elbow to your opponent's face as you block the knife hand.

Headbutt: even if you are being held in the single neck grip, you can insert a headbutt to your opponent's face as you block the slash.

Eye jab: keep inserting jabs to the eyes in rapid succession. You can do this simultaneously with other blocks or attacks.

Foot stomp: keep inserting foot stomps in rapid succession. You can do this simultaneously with other blocks or attacks. Then control the weapon hand and try to disarm, redirect or evade while continuing to hit your opponent with additional attacks.

If You're Held in a Single Neck Grip Clinch

Use this tactic when an opponent is holding you in a single neck grip clinch, and strikes at a diagonal angle from his right.

1. Block and eye jab.

2. Follow with a headbutt.

3. While your opponent is distracted, scoop the knife hand.

4. Strip and attack.

Use the tactic shown to the right when an opponent is holding you in a single neck grip clinch, and strikes at a diagonal angle from his left.

1. Block and eye jab.

2. Grab opponent's knife hand and use the knife against him.

3. If he still maintains a grip on the knife, strip and attack.

Use the tactic shown to the right when an opponent is holding you in a single neck grip clinch, and strikes at a horizontal angle from his left.

1. Block and eye jab.

2. Strip and attack.

Use the following tactic when an opponent is holding you in a single neck grip clinch, and your opponent thrusts straight toward your torso.

1. Opponent thrusts a knife to your midsection.

2. Parry and pass the knife and eye jab simultaneously.

3. Elbow your opponent's wrist.

4. Scoop and grab the knife hand.

5. Strip and attack.

Another tactic against this sort of attack must be done very quickly in order to be effective. See the steps shown to the right.

1. Move, parry and pass the knife.

2. Grab then strip and attack.

If You're Held in a Single Arm Wrap Clinch

Use this tactic when an opponent is holding you in a single arm wrap clinch, and strikes at a diagonal angle from the right.

1. Block the knife hand.

2. Follow with a headbutt.

3. Pinch the *latissimus dorsi* or armpit with your trapped hand and pull your arm out.

4. While your opponent is distracted, immediately scoop the knife hand.   5. Strip and attack.

Below is another tactic against a diagonal strike from the right when you're being held in a single arm wrap clinch.

1. Block and grab the knife hand and thrust a knee into your opponent's groin.

2. Immediately pull your arm out and elbow.

3. While your opponent is distracted, immediately scoop the knife hand.

4. Strip and attack.

Use this tactic when an opponent is holding you in a single arm wrap clinch, and strikes at a diagonal angle from the left.

1. Block and jam the knife hand as he pulls out the knife.

2. Headbutt and stomp your opponent's foot.

3. While your opponent is disoriented, pull your arm out and grab the knife hand.

4. Twist his knife hand by holding the meaty part of his thumb and turning his hand outward at the wrist. Disarm by grabbing the butt end of the knife and holding it in the ice-pick grip.

Use the following tactic when an opponent is holding you in a single arm wrap clinch, and strikes with a thrust.

1. Grab the opponent's knife hand and headbutt.

2. Still maintaining a grip on your opponent's knife hand, push it down between his legs to cut the back of his lead leg.

3. As you pull his hand up, pull your trapped arm out.

4. Twist and turn his knife hand (if he is still holding onto the knife). Gripping the meaty part of his thumb, disarm and attack.

Use the following tactic when an opponent is holding you in a single arm wrap clinch, and strikes downward with an ice pick grip.

1. Opponent begins to strike holding his knife in an ice pick grip.

2. Aiming for the wrist, block the downward strike, then immediately grab the wrist and headbutt.

3. While grabbing the knife hand at the wrist, bring it to waist level and turn it up.

4. Pinch and stomp on your opponent and pull your arm out while maintaining a grip on your opponent's knife hand.

5. Reach and grab firmly under your opponent's knife hand with the hand you just freed up. Be sure to keep your opponent's hand twisted and turned out.

6. Use the original blocking hand to strip your opponent's knife. Hold it in an ice pick grip and attack.

CHAPTER 7

Becoming a Takedown Artist

Practically all martial artists learn some type of takedown or throw. Arts like Judo, San Shou, Brazilian Jiu Jitsu and wrestling specialize in teaching and using these techniques. It is no wonder that MMA fighters who have trained extensively in those arts have an excellent advantage in taking down their opponents.

Taking down or throwing an opponent is a powerful and explosive technique that can leave your opponent psychologically shocked, physically exhausted and possibly even knocked out. These techniques require constant drilling, willing training partners and sparring practice to build your confidence in executing them. It is important to develop your timing judgement and a feel for range to perform these moves correctly. Ideally, you should be close enough to punch or grab your opponent. I recommend doing these techniques from the clinch because you can distract your opponent with strikes and control your opponent to set him up for your takedown or throw.

It is also important to distinguish between taking down your opponent in the ring and taking down your opponent in the street. Certain take downs or throws that—at worst—only knock the wind out of your opponent in the ring can break bones or kill on the pavement. When you do certain takedowns, you also risk cutting or scraping yourself on the hard street surface in ways that would only be irritating on the softer ring mat. Finally, taking down an opponent usually ends up with you grappling your opponent; that's fine in the ring where there is a referee and multiple rounds, but you want to avoid grappling—especially prolonged periods of it—when you are on the street where anything can happen.

Takedowns from the Clinch

Keeping in mind these considerations, I've focused this chapter on takedowns and throws that can be quickly executed from the clinch (for simplicity, I demonstrate with the Muay Thai clinch). These minimize the potential for damage to you while maximizing your advantage, and don't leave you vulnerable for long. You can execute takedowns when you are within kicking range, but the gap does give your opponent a little bit of time to react and defend or sprawl against your takedown.

Double-Leg Takedown I

The double-leg takedown is a move wherein you grab both of your opponent's legs and use your momentum to make him fall back. The benefit of this move over the single leg takedown is that your opponent loses his balance because you have both of his legs. Follow up the takedown by grappling or striking.

1. Begin in the clinch and (if you can) soften up your opponent with knees and other strikes.

2. Immediately drop to a squat while simultaneously keeping your back straight and your head up. To avoid a knee strike, place your arms parallel to the floor.

3. Keep your head up as you step in and grab your opponent's legs just above the knees. Thrust your body forward leading with your shoulders to take your opponent down. Your forward momentum should make him lose his balance but may have to lift your opponent to bring him down to the ground.

4. Maintain a grip on your opponent's legs to prevent him from escaping as you slide up his body.

5. Mount your opponent and attack.

Double-Leg Takedown II

There are so many variations and modifications of the double-leg takedown. In this variation, you hook your foot behind your opponent's leg to trip him and make him fall back. Follow up the takedown by grappling or striking.

1. Begin in the clinch and (if you can) soften up your opponent with knees and other strikes.

2. Immediately drop to a squat while simultaneously keeping your back straight and your head up. To avoid a knee strike, place your arms parallel to the floor. Drive your lead leg in between your opponent's legs.

3. Keep your head up as you drop your lead knee to the floor and grab behind and above the knee.

4. Hook your rear foot behind your opponent's foot to trip him.

5. After he falls, maintain a grip on your opponent's legs to prevent him from escaping as you slide up his body.

6. Mount your opponent and attack.

Single-Leg Takedown I

The single-leg takedown is a move wherein you grab one of your opponent's legs and use your momentum to make him fall back. The benefit of this move is that, although it is not as secure as when you have both of your opponent's legs, you can attack the single leg quickly and catch your opponent by surprise. You can follow up the takedown by grappling or striking.

1. Maintain the clinch on your opponent as he tries to fight his way out of it and pulls back.

2. The second he pulls his head back, drop low and grab his lead leg using one hand behind the ankle and the other behind the knee.

3. Drive your shoulder forward into your opponent's knee as you pull his leg toward you to off-balance him. Also, be quick to put your lead hand up to protect against your opponent's kick. From here you can attempt an ankle or leg submission, mount your opponent or get up and attack him while he is on the ground.

Single-Leg Takedown II

As with the double-leg takedown, there are many variations and modifications of the single-leg takedown. In this variation, you lift up your opponent's leg to make him lose balance and drop. Follow up the takedown by grappling or striking.

1. Start in the clinch.

2. Immediately drop to a squat while simultaneously keeping your back straight and your head up. To avoid a knee strike, place your arms parallel to the floor.

3. With your outside hand, snatch behind the knee and lift it up. Keep your head up and pressed into your opponent's chest.

4. Turn your body, leading with your shoulder, and drop your opponent to the floor.

Hip Throw

The hip throw requires the use of your hips as a pivot point to off-balance and throw your opponent down to the floor. Follow the throw with grappling or striking.

1. Begin in the clinch.

2. Turn your body inside and slide your arm behind your opponent's back. Be sure to drop your hips below your opponent's hips.

3. Use your hips to lift and toss your opponent over you. Be sure to pull his arm as you toss him over.

4. Maintain a grip on your opponent's arm and pin him with your knee.

Neck Throw

The neck throw is basically like a hip throw where you wrap your arm around your opponent's neck, instead of under the armpit, while using your hips as a pivot point to off-balance and throw your opponent down to the floor. Follow the throw with grappling or striking.

1. Begin in the clinch.

2. Turn your body inside and hook your arm around your opponent's head. Be sure to drop your hips below your opponent's hips.

3. Use your hips to lift and toss your opponent over you. Be sure to pull his arm as you toss him over.

4. Pin your opponent with your knee.

Take the Back and Choke

Sometimes you can end the fight with a grappling hold while remaining upright. With this combination technique, you pass your opponent's limbs so that you can grab a hold of your opponent from behind and choke him out.

1. As you clinch your opponent, he tries to push you away at the hips.

2. While maintaining a grip on his neck, grab his triceps, strip his arm from your hips and pull it in.

3. As you pull his arm in, spin around him and take your opponent's back. Wrap the arm you used to pull your opponent's arm around his throat.

4. Tighten your grip and choke your opponent out. If he is taller than you, kick the back of one of his legs to bring him down to a more manageable height.

Defending Against the Clinch to a Rear Ankle Grab Takedown

This technique combination allows you to drop your opponent onto his face and immediately gain the upper hand. To do this effectively, you must be as fast and slippery as an eel to pass your opponent's limbs and get behind him.

1. Your opponent has you in the clinch.

2. Dip your head to the outside, under your opponent's arm as you step behind him. Push down and check your opponent's other arm, simultaneously.

3. Maintain a grip on your opponent's arm and secure it with your free hand as you go behind him.

4. Immediately drop, grab his ankles and pull them as you push forward behind his legs.

5. Take your opponent's back as soon as he falls to the ground.

Bear Hug Takedown

While defending yourself in the clinch, you can find an opportunity to not only strike back at your opponent, but also take him down. With this bear hug takedown you lock down one of his arms to minimize your opponent's ability to retaliate. Once you have him locked, immediately take him down.

1. Your opponent has you in the clinch.

2. Push up and back to loosen up the clinch.

3. Then wrap around the arm with one arm and wrap around the waist with the other.

Step 3 viewed from another angle.

4. Squeeze your opponent's waist and apply downward pressure.

Defending Against the Clinch to a Rear Leg Trip

With this takedown, you spin behind your opponent and trip him backward. This is especially effective when your opponent does not have a strong clinch hold on you.

1. Your opponent has you in the clinch.

2. Dip your head to the outside under your opponent's arm as you step behind him. Push down and check your opponent's other arm, simultaneously.

3. Maintain a grip on your opponent's arm and continue moving around him. Set up your lead leg behind him and push him back to trip him.

4. As soon as he falls to the floor, take the top position.

Defending Against the Clinch to a Single-Leg Sweep

This takedown allows you to drop your opponent with a front-leg sweep. Punching or pushing your opponent's face, as well as lifting your opponent's leg up high, are both necessary to off-balance your opponent in this technique.

1. Your opponent has you in the clinch.

2. Push up and back on his face to loosen the clinch and step forward...

3. And then drop and lift up your opponent's leg to off-balance him.

4. Turn and sweep your opponent onto his back.

Preventing the Takedown

You must master defending against throws and takedowns just like you would master defense against punches and kicks. Aside from protecting yourself, mastering defenses against throws and takedowns allows you to counterattack so that you are not only on the defensive when your opponent attempts these techniques against you.

Drop Stance

Dropping your stance is a good reaction whenever you see your opponent drop his body to rush you. It's key that you keep your hands available to hook them under his armpits in case he gets inside. Also, be quick to bring your hand up to defend against any punches.

While keeping your hands up to protect against strikes, drop very low. Immediately return to your fighting stance.

Sprawl

To defend against a takedown with a sprawl requires good timing. As your opponent comes for you, push down on his head. Spread your base out so that he can't grab the backs of your legs and use your weight to keep pushing his head down to the mat.

As your opponent comes for you, push down on his head. Widen your base so that he can't grab the backs of your legs and use your weight to keep pushing his head down to the mat.

Knee the Head

This offensive technique accompanies the defensive sprawl technique described above. The reason kneeing the head works as a counter here is because your opponent's forward momentum will make your knee strike land twice as hard. A knee strike here takes advantage of your opponent's moment of vulnerability and can end the fight immediately.

Knee your opponent's head as you're pushing it down.

Knee your opponent's head as he comes in for the sprawl.

Redirect or Push Away

The next best thing to striking back at your opponent is evading your opponent's attack completely. By redirecting and pushing away, you evade and escape or position yourself to better attack your opponent while he is off balance.

1. Face your opponent and as he makes an attempt for a leg take-down, block your opponent's face as you step to the side. Here you can knee, punch, or pull your opponent's hair or ear...

2. Or, continue pushing him away so that your opponent falls to the ground.

Push Back

Sometimes you want to meet force with force. With the push back, you are confronting your opponent's forward momentum and forcing him back. This move can throw him off balance, allowing you to grapple or strike.

Face your opponent and as he makes an attempt for a leg takedown, block your opponent on his shoulders and push him back "up." It's vital that you keep your legs away from his hands so that he doesn't get a grip on them and latch on tight.

Variation: If your opponent is closer or your timing is very good, you can also block your opponent before he gets lower to the ground. Block him at the shoulders and push him back "up."

Preventing the Takedown on the Street

Sometimes life or death situations will require a more violent and aggressive tactic. Add these basic techniques to your repertoire to defend against an opponent attempting to take you down—especially if you are unable to perform the more conventional tactics in the heat of the moment.

All of the takedowns and throws in this chapter, including the defenses and counters, can be used in the streets. If your life is on the line, or you are fighting multiple opponents where speed is of the essence, you can use dirty streetfighting techniques such as the eye gouge, hair pull, and ear pull to stay upright, and in a position to end the fight quickly.

CHAPTER 8

Becoming a Ground Fighting Pro

Without a doubt, today's fighter needs ground fighting skills to survive in a modern-day hand-to-hand combat scenario. The popularity of MMA is evidence of that. Ground fighting is not just a fighting style, but also a combat range. In the ground-fighting range, you will be fighting an opponent with minimal space between the two of you. Technical skills, good reflexes and bursts of raw power will be decisive in emerging victorious from a fight on the ground. The risks are compounded when you add a weapon to the mix. Pure ground fighters and MMA fighters have to always be aware of the potential that they will need to fight in the streets where there are no rules. Because we fight the way we train, it can be very easy for a fighter accustomed to fighting on the ground to take the fight there when his or her life is on the line. A good ground fighter who does that still has an advantage against an opponent, but that advantage can be thrown out the window once the opponent pulls out a knife or calls his friends to help him. That is why a ground fighter should always add elements of unpredictability, weapons and street encounters into their training. It will not only add to your fight game in the ring or the mat as a form of cross-training, but it may also save your life one day.

Basic Grappling Positions

The basic grappling positions are the mount, the guard, the side control, the knee-on-the-chest, the *kesa gatame* and the north-south position. A good understanding and application of these six positions will make you an incredible fighter. Out of these six positions, hundreds of variations have evolved.

Mount

The mount is a position that allows you to sit or rest your body on top of your opponent. This dominant position gives you a strong upper hand against your opponent whether you are striking or going for a grappling hold.

In the mount, your knees are right under your opponent's armpits. Drop your weight onto your opponent's chest.

In the high mount, your knees are higher up on your opponent's armpits, forcing his shoulders upward. Drop your weight onto your opponent's chest.

Hooks in—sink your weight onto your opponent to keep the mount and hook your feet around his legs to maintain the mount. You'll have more control but less maneuverability. Once you've secured your position, resume the mount or high mount position.

Guard

The guard is a position that allows you to control your opponent's arms and neck while subduing him with your legs around his torso. From this position you can have your legs locked or unlocked, and you are also able to shift your feet over different parts of your opponent's body. Another benefit of the guard is that it allows you to easily move around your opponent. There are many types of guards, but for the purposes of this book, I will focus on the closed and open guard positions. Closed guard is when you have your feet locked around your opponent's waist for a secure hold. Open guard is when your feet are unlocked and braced on different parts of your opponent's body; this position sacrifices a secure hold for increased mobility.

Closed Guard—Maintain grips on one of your opponent's arms and his head to keep him down.

Open Guard—Maintain grips on your opponent's wrists to maneuver him into a position you can attack from.

Side Control

The side control is a position that allows you to lay your body on top of your opponent, perpendicularly. This dominant position gives you a strong upper hand against your opponent, especially because it lets you neutralize their arms, legs and movement at the same time.

Side control allows you to pin your opponent with your chest and neutralize his arms and legs.

Knee-on-Chest

The knee-on-chest is a position that allows you to pin your opponent on the chest with your knee. While you certainly have opportunities to put your opponent in grappling holds from here, the main benefit of this position is that it allows you to strike and easily shift to another position.

Kesa Gatame

The *kesa gatame* is a dominant position that allows you to press your weight onto your opponent as you lock your opponent's arm and neck. From this position you can strike and force your opponent's submission, and he is especially vulnerable to chokes and arm locks.

A knee on the chest can be very painful. Balance with your knee pointing into your opponent's chest and brace with your standing leg.

Wrap your arm around your opponent's head, place your body up under his armpit, and sink your weight onto his chest.

North-South

The north-south is a position that allows you to press your body weight on your opponent beneath you while controlling his legs or arms. From this position, your opponent is especially vulnerable to knees to the head.

Place your body over your opponent's body to minimize his movements and control his arms. From here you can strike, force him to submit with locks or chokes, or transition to another position.

Defense and Escape

Here are some main points to remember when you're defending yourself on the ground from a variety of positions:

- Cover your face as much as possible with your hand or by moving your upper body or head away from oncoming strikes.
- Practice and spar your ground fighting techniques to the point that they become intuitive and you are constantly moving and reacting, looking for opportunities to hit or force a submission.
- Whenever you are changing or maintaining positions, aim to create or compress space. Creating space can allow you to escape certain holds or open up opportunities for you to hit or force your opponent's submission, while compressing space can allow you to hold and control your opponent.
- Be relaxed and learn your techniques well enough to know how to set them up, apply them effectively, and know the possible counters and re-counters to your techniques.
- Your body should be like an antenna; be aware of your limbs and of what your opponents are trying to do even when you can't see what they are trying to do.

Escape from the Mount

Escape your opponent's mount to put him in your guard.

1. Scoot to your right side and push inside his left thigh. Use your elbows to create space. Push with your hands as well, if you need to.

2. Bring your right knee up to your elbow and hook it over his leg.

3. With your leg hooked over, pivot your body and pull your other leg out so that you can put your opponent into a closed guard.

Another escape technique is to move into an *upa* (bridge) position to escape your opponent's mount.

1. Grab your opponent's right arm while bracing your free hand on your opponent's left hip.

2. Bridge up and toss your opponent diagonally and over you. Your aim is to get him completely off of you, but you may end up in his guard. If you end up in your opponent's guard, proceed to escape his guard as well (see below).

Escape from the Guard

Escape from your opponent's closed guard by leaning back.

1. Lean back while keeping your hands on his waist.

2. Slide back and wrap your arms around his legs to prevent him from putting you back in his guard position.

3. Holding tight to your opponent, crawl up to the mount or take the side position.

Escape your opponent's closed guard by stepping to the side.

If your opponent doesn't have a solid closed guard, you can simply stand up. While standing, grip your opponent's ankles and pull them to one side to clear your way. Step forward and drop your knee on your opponent's chest.

Escape from your
opponent's closed guard
with a knee pass.

1. Keep your head and back straight with your hands on his hips while you break his loose closed guard.

2. Insert your elbows into his thighs to open him up.

3. Slide your right knee over the thigh you "elbowed" and then step your other leg over his leg.

4. Maintain downward pressure on his hips as you move up and put your opponent into the side control position.

Escape from the Side Control

Escape your opponent's side control and transition to guard.

1. Tuck your arms tight to your chest so that your opponent isn't able to force you to submit, then violently push up with your hands as you scoot your body outward.

2. Turn into him and put him in your guard.

Escape from the Knee-on-Chest

Escape your opponent's knee-on-chest by pushing the knee.

1. Turn into your opponent's knee and place both of your hands on his knee. Then scoot your body outward and push the knee off.

2. If he loses his balance, turn and put him into the guard position.

Escape from the *Kesa Gatame*

Escape your opponent's *kesa gatame* by rolling over.

1. Wrap your arms around your opponent's ribs and turn toward your opponent to help generate leverage and momentum.

2. Bridge and throw your opponent over your body with both of your arms still wrapped around him.

3. Turn into your opponent to complete the roll and take the top position.

Escape your opponent's *kesa gatame* by taking your opponent's back.

1. Push up on your opponent's face.

2. As you push up, turn into your opponent to create more space. With his hold on you broken, slide your arm out and grip your opponent's back. Continue sliding out diagonally until you're behind him and can take his back.

North-South

Escape from under the north-south position by rolling over the top.

1. Keep your arms in tight so that they won't be used to force you to submit and push up on your opponent's waist. Using your *upa*, tuck your knees into the space to push him further up and away.

2. Grab your opponent's wrists and put your feet under his armpits, then push back with your legs.

3. Roll over with the momentum and put your opponent in the mount, side control or knee-on-chest.

Ground Fighting Submissions—Chokes

The main grappling holds involve the neck area or the limbs. Chokeholds and limb locks can be done from every position in grappling. Chokeholds obstruct your opponent's airway or blood flow to the brain and render him unconscious.

If streetfighting, note your vulnerability—your back is exposed to your opponent's friends and your opponent could be accessing a weapon with a free hand. The steps below illustrate how to perform a neck lock from the mount.

1. Push down on your opponent's hands and slide your arm around the back of his neck. Then push his arm in between your bodies to use during your choke.

2. Press your body down with his arm pressed against his neck and lock your arms together in a lever grip. Squeeze your elbows together to choke him out.

If your opponent is protecting his arm in *kesa gatame*, go for a choke. If streetfighting, be aware of the possibility that your opponent could access a weapon with a free hand. The photos below show how to perform a choke from *kesa gatame*.

1. From *kesa gatame* position, push your opponent's trapped arm in between your bodies.

2. Then wrap your far arm around the back of your opponent's neck.

3. Press your body down with his arm pressed against his neck and lock your arms together in a lever grip. Squeeze your elbows together to choke him out in the *kesa gatame* position. Or, sprawl out and continue choking.

Choking from the open guard allows you to end the fight without having to shift your body too much, thus minimizing the possibility that you will lose the guard. The photos below show how to perform a triangle choke from the open guard.

1. Manipulate your opponent by gripping his wrists.

2. Place one of his arms in between your chests.

3. Place your foot on his hip and turn your body while simultaneously throwing your leg over his head.

4. Lock your legs in a "figure-4" around his head, pull his trapped arm tightly across his throat. Squeeze your knees, arch your hips and pull down on your opponent's head.

The guillotine is a devastating choke that can quickly end the fight once you have your arm locked in. Mind your opponent's ability to access a weapon with a free hand while performing this choke.

The following photos illustrate how to perform a guillotine from the guard.

1. Hold your opponent in the guard position.

2. Shift your body forward.

3. Wrap one of your arms around his neck.

4. Lock your hands with your arm wrapped around his neck and then pull up against his chin while arching back.

If your opponent is blocking successfully and is on the verge of escaping, go for the razor choke to quickly end the fight.

The following photos illustrate how to perform a knee-on-chest to razor choke.

1. From the knee-on-chest position, grab the back of your opponent's head with one arm.

2. Place your other hand behind neck.

3. Slide your leg forward for leverage as you drop your weight on him.

4. Squeeze with your arms to choke him out.

Pulling off the choke from north-south is a bit unusual, and may catch your opponent off guard. Beware of your opponent's ability to grab you if you try to disengage to face other attackers.

The following photos illustrate how to perform a choke from north-south.

1. Hold your opponent in the north-south position.

2. Drop your hips and move to the side so that you can free up some space to operate.

3. Wrap your arm around your opponent's neck, lock it with your free arm and squeeze.

Ground Fighting Submissions—Limb attacks

Arm locks can hyperextend, hyperflex or hyperrotate the elbow joints and the shoulder joints depending on the placement of the body and the position you are in during execution. Full-body leverage and secure grips are necessary for a secure and effective arm lock. When done quickly, forcefully and aggressively, you can cause damage to muscles, tendons and ligaments, dislocate joints and even fracture bones.

The arm bar is a dynamic and devastating attack, requiring timing and speed to perform without losing the mount position. Beware of other attackers or surprise weapons. The following photos illustrate how to apply an arm bar from the mount.

1. Push down on your opponent's face while you grip his arm at the triceps and pull it up and tight to your body. Lean all of your weight on your pushing hand, using it as a pivot point, so that you can swing your left leg around and over his head. (Not shown.)

2. While retaining and squeezing his arm with your legs, lean back and arch your hips upwards.

The key lock is a safe attack to perform if you do not want to risk losing your mount position, and your opponent is making it difficult for you to do a choke. The following photos illustrate how to perform a key lock from the mount.

1. Reach across his body with your hand, grab his wrist and then push down on his elbow with the other hand.

2. Slide the hand that you used to push his elbow under his pinned arm and grip your pinning wrist. Turn his arm in a "painting" motion, using it like a brush to paint the floor.

The *kimura* is great for when you cannot or do not want to perform a choke. The following photos illustrate how to perform a *kimura* from the guard.

1. In the guard position, grab his wrist.

2. Reach across with your other hand to "grapevine" around his arm and grab your own wrist.

3. Lift his arm and twist it.

The photos to the right illustrate how to perform a top key lock from the north-south position.

This lock may catch your opponent off guard as many fighters will expect you to rest or try to transition to a "better" position. When your

1. From the north-south position, grab your opponent's arm at the wrist as you put the weight of your chest on his head.

opponent tries to escape, you can quickly take advantage by doing a simple key lock on your opponent's arm. In a streetfighting situation, you have the advantage of being on top and raining knees to the head, along with being able to damage your opponent's limb. However, be mindful of multiple attackers and surprise weapons.

The photos to the right illustrate how to perform an arm bar from the knee-on-chest position.

The arm bar from the knee-on-chest is effective when your opponent brings up his hands to defend his face from your strikes. The strength of this move is its swift application. It will not totally incapacitate your opponent like a choke would, but it will limit your opponent's fighting effectiveness. Once you have mastered this move, you can perform it even more quickly than the choke. As always in a streetfighting situation, beware of multiple attackers and surprise weapons.

2. As you press your weight on him, turn your body towards the pinned arm and slide your free hand underneath and grab your pinning wrist. Squeeze your arms together and twist your opponent's arm.

1. Punch your opponent in the face.

2. Push down on it with your other hand, as your punching hand grabs his arm at the triceps and pulls it up and tight against your body.

3. Lean all of your weight through your pushing hand and use it as a pivot point to swing your left leg around and over the top of his head.

4. Retain his arm, squeezing it with your legs and fall back.

Striking in Grappling

Striking in grappling has two pretty straightforward goals: Knock your opponent out or set your opponent up for a submission. Some strikes are better suited for some positions than others (knees are most practical in the north-south and side control positions). It's good to practice strike combinations from different grappling positions so that they can become as fluid and as overwhelming as a boxer's combination in the ring.

Popular Striking Combinations in Grappling

These are some popular striking combinations from different grappling positions.

Combination 1 (from the mount):

1. Jab

2. Cross   Cont.

3. Hook

4. Hammerfist

5. Elbow

Combination 2
(from guard):

1. Jab

2. Cross

3. Grab your opponent's head, pull him down and elbow.

Combination 3
(from *kesa gatame*):

1. Hook

2. Elbow

Combination 4
(from side control):

1. Hammerfist

2. Elbow

3. Knee Ribs

Combination 5
(from north-south):

1. Knee Head and Shoulders

2. Elbow Ribs

Combination 6
(from knee-on-chest):

1. Jab

2. Cross

3. Hammerfist

4. Elbow

Facing a Standing Opponent When You're on the Ground

A vulnerable position to be in is when you're on your back and your opponent is standing above you. Although your main goal when you're in that situation is to get up as soon as possible to face off your opponent, you must do it safely; always aware that your opponent will try to attack you while you are in a compromised position. Practice moving away and toward your opponent while you're on the ground as he tries to attack you. Also add different kicks to your movements so that you can turn the tables on an opponent who drops his guard while trying to attack you.

Moving away—Scoot away left, right, forward and backward with one hand covering your face.

Side kick.

A front kick can be aimed at the opponent's knee, groin, stomach or face.

Heel stomp the top of the foot.

Heel strike to the inner thigh.

Sweeping—place your foot behind your opponent's lead ankle and push on their knee with your kicking foot.

Ground Fighting Defense in the Street

Fighting on the ground in the street is dangerous because the fight can end quickly—and badly—for you if your opponent is a trained grappler or if friends accompany your opponent. In situations like this, where your life is on the line, extreme measures have to be taken, such as:

- Biting
- Headbutting
- Eye gouging
- Pinching vulnerable body parts

- Breaking the fingers
- Punching the groin
- Stomping the feet
- Raking the face

Basic Techniques for Escaping Positions

These solutions illustrate how the previously listed extreme measures can be employed to escape from various precarious positions.

Escaping the mount—punch the groin.

Escaping the guard—punch the groin or hammerfist the face.

Escaping *kesa gatame*—pull the hair or finger jab the eye or throat.

Escaping side control—pull on the ear or the hair and elbow the face.

Escaping knee-on-chest—punch or elbow the groin.

Escaping north-south—break the finger or push your opponent up and knee his head.

Ground Fighting an Opponent with a Knife

Grappling with an armed opponent while you are empty-handed is one of the worst streetfighting scenarios to be in because your life is on the line. You have a severely limited range of counters that you can successfully perform. You also stand a good chance of being seriously cut if you survive. And your adrenaline will be pumping to the point where your body, in its "fight or flight" mode, will have you reacting on animal instincts.

Preparing for all types of scenarios means devoting time in your training to some basic techniques you can learn and practice consistently until they are ingrained in your fighting system so that even when you are relying on animal instincts, you will be able to pull the moves off.

When fighting for your life, a few key points are relevant:

- Perform your techniques with violence and aggression.
- Aim to use whatever is on your person or in your environment as a defensive shield to cover your face and limbs while your strike back.
- Constantly move and hit your opponent whether it's with single strikes or combinations. Use the extreme measures listed previously.
- If you can't move away, redirect your opponent's attacks with parries. Do not focus on disarming your opponent; your focus should be on *escaping*. Disarming your opponent is easier to do when you've hurt him before the disarm attempt.
- Prepare to see blood, yours or your opponents, and condition yourself to keep on fighting, no matter what.

Part of the reason why you try to avoid fighting on the ground in the streets is because you don't want to be surprised by your opponent's weapon once you are rolling in the ground. This is because of the extreme damage a knife can cause in such close quarters. For situations like this, you need to be able to block the knife attack while escaping your opponent's attack. Unfortunately, that might mean taking punches to the face while you try to block, disarm or redirect your opponent's knife. That also means fighting back quickly and decisively with the necessary amount of aggression if you want to survive.

Defending Against a Knife-Wielding Grappler Who Is in Your Guard

Being in the guard against an opponent with a knife is extremely dangerous because your groin, stomach and thighs (where the femoral artery is located) are completely exposed to your opponent. You want to block your opponent's knife hand once he strikes but you might also be better off simply letting go of the guard and getting up to your feet.

1. Your opponent is mounted and stabs down. Block with your left forearm and jab his eye.

2. Turn the knife hand at the wrist as the blade rests against your forearm, grab his wrist with your other hand as you strip the knife from the hilt.

Defending Against a Knife-Wielding Grappler Who Has You in Guard

Escaping your opponent's guard just got more difficult now that he is slashing and stabbing at you. Your only slight advantage is that you are more stable as you fight back and block. Block the knife and be aggressive in your counterattack.

1. Punch your opponent's groin as you block his slashing strike. With your punching hand, sweep the knife hand away.

2. Grab the meaty part of your opponent's knife hand and twist and turn it away from you. Strip the knife from your opponent.

Defending Against a Knife-Wielding Grappler from the Mount

Being mounted by a knife-wielding opponent is one of the worst positions to be in. Your face, armpits and limbs are completely exposed to your opponent's slashing and stabbing. Keeping your hands up is vital to your survival and you may have to opt for getting cuts on your arms to getting the same cuts on your face.

1. Your opponent is mounted and stabs downwards. Parry it to the side so that it stabs your opponent's thigh.

2. With your left hand, grab the meaty part of his knife hand and twist it up and back violently. Strip the knife with your other hand.

CHAPTER 9

The Complete Warrior
Workout Program

GOAL: Prepare to be fight-ready for the streets or the ring after learning the basics.

It is recommended that you have at least six months of steady and continuous training in mixed martial arts to lay a foundation of basics that you can rely upon.

The goals for the following three months are flexible and can be adjusted if you have more or less time to train. For example, if you only have six weeks to prepare, then aim to achieve the goals of Month One in the first two weeks, the goals of Month Two in the next two weeks and the goals of Month Three in the last two weeks.

Month One

The purpose of Month One is to supercharge your body. Starting from a base level of at least six months of steady and continuous training in techniques, you will begin a boot camp regimen to give a boost to the attributes you need to be a top fighter: strength, stamina, speed, agility and flexibility. From a mental perspective, you will also lay a foundation for your fight strategy. Your fighting strategy can involve research, studying different fighting styles or reviewing video footage.

Month One regimen:

- Cardio (run, jump rope, jumping jacks, stationary bike, etc.) three times a week.
- Improve flexibility through stretching.
- Upper body exercises three times a week.
- Lower body exercises three times a week.
- Core exercises (crunches, bicycle sit-ups, superman, plank, etc.) three times a week.
- If you're competing, review the rules.
- Plan your strategy for the streets based on the safeties and dangers of your environment or for a fight based on the rules of the event. For both scenarios, make an honest assessment of your skills.
- Solidify basics that you should know in your rank or belt level (movement, strikes, escapes, submissions, etc.).
- Specialized drills and sparring (focus on particular drills to hone certain aspects of your game).
- Begin tracking data in the training log that begins on page 107 of this book.

If you require additional space to record your notes, visit the *Mixed Martial Arts Fighting Techniques* page at **www.tuttlepublishing.com** to access a PDF file containing expanded training log sheets that you can print as needed.

Month Two

The purpose of Month Two is to fine-tune your techniques and attributes and to fix your deficiencies. You are also in a prime position to benefit from your sparring sessions, since you are now in, or approaching, top form as a streetfighter. Aim to fine-tune your strengths and fix your weaknesses by the end of the month.

Month Two regimen:

- Continue cardio, flexibility, upper body, lower body, and core exercises.
- Improve speed and delivery of your techniques.
- Cross train with other martial arts or sports to enhance other attributes (timing, speed, targeting, movement, etc.).
- Continue specialized drills and sparring.
- Add regular sparring.
- Refine strategy for a variety of opponents in different scenarios and try to find out as much as you can about the opponent(s) you expect to face.

Month Three

The purpose of Month Three is to get yourself close to peaking and maintain that edge until the day of your fight. At this point, you want to continue fine-tuning and fixing without going overboard and burning out.

Month Three regimen:

- Continue cardio, flexibility, upper body, lower body, and core exercises.
- Continue training techniques and escapes to improve speed and mastery.
- Continue specialized sparring (practice escaping, holding position, etc.).
- Continue regular sparring (improve submission times) up until two weeks before the fight. No heavy sparring after this point.

Two Weeks Before the Fight

At this point, you should be feeling primed and confident. Continue that path and make the final preparations, mentally, physically and logistically for the fight.

- Aim to be at near peak in terms of your flexibility, speed, stamina, agility and strength.
- Know your opponent's fight game strategy (if possible), as well as your own strengths and weaknesses.
- Prepare gear and other logistics for fight night.

The Week of the Fight

Now you are ready to fight. This is where your mental game kicks in. Trust your training and your trainers. You have put in the work and are ready for the challenge. You have done the hard part because of your regimen and your discipline and you're ready to win. No matter what happens, though, give 100% and be proud that you had the guts to step in and fight.

- Spar light, focusing mostly on specialized sparring.
- Less cardio and calisthenics—maintenance drills and exercises only.
- Use visualization.
- Be calm and confident.

Week 1

Weight: _____   Target weight: _____

Class & Training Log	Monday	Tuesday	Wednesday	Thursday	Friday	Saturday	Sunday

STRETCH: 5 – 7 MINUTES

CARDIO: _____ miles / min   STRATEGY:

UPPER BODY: _____ ___sets ___reps

_____ ___sets ___reps

_____ ___sets ___reps   BASIC TECHNIQUES:

_____ ___sets ___reps

LOWER BODY: _____ ___sets ___reps

_____ ___sets ___reps

_____ ___sets ___reps   BASIC DRILLS:

_____ ___sets ___reps

CORE: _____ ___sets ___reps

SPARRING ASSESSMENT: (pros/cons of your matches; what worked, what needs work)

Week 2

Weight: _____   Target weight: _____

Class & Training Log	Monday	Tuesday	Wednesday	Thursday	Friday	Saturday	Sunday

STRETCH: 5 – 7 MINUTES

CARDIO: _____ miles / min   STRATEGY:

UPPER BODY: _____ ___sets ___reps

_____ ___sets ___reps

_____ ___sets ___reps   BASIC TECHNIQUES:

_____ ___sets ___reps

LOWER BODY: _____ ___sets ___reps

_____ ___sets ___reps

_____ ___sets ___reps   BASIC DRILLS:

_____ ___sets ___reps

CORE: _____ ___sets ___reps

SPARRING ASSESSMENT: (pros/cons of your matches; what worked, what needs work)

Week 3

Weight: _____ Target weight: _____

Class & Training Log	Monday	Tuesday	Wednesday	Thursday	Friday	Saturday	Sunday

STRETCH: 5 – 7 MINUTES

CARDIO: _____ miles / min   STRATEGY:

UPPER BODY: _____ ___sets ___reps

_____ ___sets ___reps

_____ ___sets ___reps   BASIC TECHNIQUES:

_____ ___sets ___reps

LOWER BODY: _____ ___sets ___reps

_____ ___sets ___reps

_____ ___sets ___reps   BASIC DRILLS:

_____ ___sets ___reps

CORE: _____ ___sets ___reps

SPARRING ASSESSMENT: (pros/cons of your matches; what worked, what needs work)

Week 4

Weight: _____ Target weight: _____

Class & Training Log	Monday	Tuesday	Wednesday	Thursday	Friday	Saturday	Sunday

STRETCH: 5 – 7 MINUTES

CARDIO: _____ miles / min   STRATEGY:

UPPER BODY: _____ ___sets ___reps

_____ ___sets ___reps

_____ ___sets ___reps   BASIC TECHNIQUES:

_____ ___sets ___reps

LOWER BODY: _____ ___sets ___reps

_____ ___sets ___reps

_____ ___sets ___reps   BASIC DRILLS:

_____ ___sets ___reps

CORE: _____ ___sets ___reps

SPARRING ASSESSMENT: (pros/cons of your matches; what worked, what needs work)

Week 5

Weight: _____   Target weight: _____

	Monday	Tuesday	Wednesday	Thursday	Friday	Saturday	Sunday
Class & Training Log							

STRETCH: 5 – 7 MINUTES

CARDIO: _____ miles / min   STRATEGY:

UPPER BODY: _____ ___sets ___reps

_____ ___sets ___reps

_____ ___sets ___reps   TECHNIQUES & DRILLS TO IMPROVE SPEED &

_____ ___sets ___reps   DELIVERY:

LOWER BODY: _____ ___sets ___reps

_____ ___sets ___reps

_____ ___sets ___reps   CROSS TRAINING EFFECTIVENESS:

_____ ___sets ___reps   (what you did, how it helped, etc.)

CORE: _____ ___sets ___reps

SPARRING ASSESSMENT: (pros/cons of your matches; what worked, what needs work)

Week 6

Weight: _____   Target weight: _____

	Monday	Tuesday	Wednesday	Thursday	Friday	Saturday	Sunday
Class & Training Log							

STRETCH: 5 – 7 MINUTES

CARDIO: _____ miles / min   STRATEGY:

UPPER BODY: _____ ___sets ___reps

_____ ___sets ___reps

_____ ___sets ___reps   TECHNIQUES & DRILLS TO IMPROVE SPEED &

_____ ___sets ___reps   DELIVERY:

LOWER BODY: _____ ___sets ___reps

_____ ___sets ___reps

_____ ___sets ___reps   CROSS TRAINING EFFECTIVENESS:

_____ ___sets ___reps   (what you did, how it helped, etc.)

CORE: _____ ___sets ___reps

SPARRING ASSESSMENT: (pros/cons of your matches; what worked, what needs work)

Week 7

Weight: _____ Target weight: _____

	Monday	Tuesday	Wednesday	Thursday	Friday	Saturday	Sunday
Class & Training Log							

STRETCH: 5 – 7 MINUTES

CARDIO: _____ miles / min   STRATEGY:

UPPER BODY: _____ ___sets ___reps

_____ ___sets ___reps

_____ ___sets ___reps   TECHNIQUES & DRILLS:

_____ ___sets ___reps

LOWER BODY: _____ ___sets ___reps

_____ ___sets ___reps

_____ ___sets ___reps   CROSS TRAINING EFFECTIVENESS:

_____ ___sets ___reps   (what you did, how it helped, etc.)

CORE: _____ ___sets ___reps

SPARRING ASSESSMENT: (pros/cons of your matches; what worked, what needs work)

Week 8

Weight: _____ Target weight: _____

	Monday	Tuesday	Wednesday	Thursday	Friday	Saturday	Sunday
Class & Training Log							

STRETCH: 5 – 7 MINUTES

CARDIO: _____ miles / min   STRATEGY:

UPPER BODY: _____ ___sets ___reps

_____ ___sets ___reps

_____ ___sets ___reps   TECHNIQUES & DRILLS:

_____ ___sets ___reps

LOWER BODY: _____ ___sets ___reps

_____ ___sets ___reps

_____ ___sets ___reps   CROSS TRAINING EFFECTIVENESS:

_____ ___sets ___reps   (what you did, how it helped, etc.)

CORE: _____ ___sets ___reps

SPARRING ASSESSMENT: (pros/cons of your matches; what worked, what needs work)

Week 9

Weight: _____   Target weight: _____

	Monday	Tuesday	Wednesday	Thursday	Friday	Saturday	Sunday
Class & Training Log							

STRETCH: 5 – 7 MINUTES

CARDIO: _____ miles / min   STRATEGY:

UPPER BODY: _____ ___sets ___reps

_____ ___sets ___reps

_____ ___sets ___reps   TECHNIQUES & DRILLS:

_____ ___sets ___reps

LOWER BODY: _____ ___sets ___reps

_____ ___sets ___reps

_____ ___sets ___reps   CROSS TRAINING EFFECTIVENESS:

_____ ___sets ___reps   (what you did, how it helped, etc.)

CORE: _____ ___sets ___reps

SPARRING ASSESSMENT: (pros/cons of your matches; what worked, what needs work)

Week 10

Weight: _____   Target weight: _____

	Monday	Tuesday	Wednesday	Thursday	Friday	Saturday	Sunday
Class & Training Log							

STRETCH: 5 – 7 MINUTES

CARDIO: _____ miles / min   STRATEGY:

UPPER BODY: _____ ___sets ___reps

_____ ___sets ___reps

_____ ___sets ___reps   TECHNIQUES & DRILLS:

_____ ___sets ___reps

LOWER BODY: _____ ___sets ___reps

_____ ___sets ___reps

_____ ___sets ___reps   CROSS TRAINING EFFECTIVENESS:

_____ ___sets ___reps   (what you did, how it helped, etc.)

CORE: _____ ___sets ___reps

SPARRING ASSESSMENT: (pros/cons of your matches; what worked, what needs work)

Week 11

Weight: _____ Target weight: _____

Class & Training Log	Monday	Tuesday	Wednesday	Thursday	Friday	Saturday	Sunday

STRETCH: 5 – 7 MINUTES

CARDIO: _____ miles / min   STRATEGY:

UPPER BODY: _____ ___sets ___reps

_____ ___sets ___reps

_____ ___sets ___reps   BASIC TECHNIQUES:

_____ ___sets ___reps

LOWER BODY: _____ ___sets ___reps

_____ ___sets ___reps

_____ ___sets ___reps   CROSS TRAINING EFFECTIVENESS:

_____ ___sets ___reps   (what you did, how it helped, etc.)

CORE: _____ ___sets ___reps

LIGHT & FOCUSED SPARRING ASSESSMENT:

Week 12

Weight: _____ Target weight: _____

Class & Training Log	Monday	Tuesday	Wednesday	Thursday	Friday	Saturday	Sunday

STRETCH: 5 – 7 MINUTES

CARDIO: _____ miles / min   STRATEGY:

UPPER BODY: _____ ___sets ___reps

_____ ___sets ___reps

_____ ___sets ___reps   BASIC TECHNIQUES:

_____ ___sets ___reps

LOWER BODY: _____ ___sets ___reps

_____ ___sets ___reps

_____ ___sets ___reps   LOGISTICS:

_____ ___sets ___reps

CORE: _____ ___sets ___reps

LIGHT & FOCUSED SPARRING ASSESSMENT: